CONFIDENCE WORKS

...ssful life and business ...e many and varied. She is GM... ...vsite life coach and broadcasts regularly on radio and television and has been the resident psycho-therapist for Channel 4's *Espresso* and agony aunt for *Yes!* magazine. She also acts as a counselling adviser to Channel 4's *Big Brother* and more recently as the life coach and counsellor for Channel 4's *Model Behaviour*. Gladeana is a BACP Senior Registered Practitioner and Accredited Counsellor, a BABCP Accredited Cognitive-Behavioural Psychotherapist, who is UKCP and UKRC (ind. Couns) registered. Gladeana's training includes Diplomas in Cognitive-Behavioural Therapy, Crisis Counselling and Management Studies.

A prolific writer, Gladeana has written, co-authored, edited or contributed to some 16 publications, the most recent of which was *Coping with Life's Traumas*. She is a part-time senior lecturer on the postgraduate and Masters programmes at the University of East London and is managing editor of *Stress News*, associate editor of the *Counselling and Psychotherapy Journal* and sits on the editorial boards of various professional journals. She is a regular speaker on the conference circuit and is co-director of both the Centre for Stress Management and Centre for Coaching.

Overcoming Common Problems Series

For a full list of titles please contact
Sheldon Press, Marylebone Road, London NW1 4DU

Overcoming Common Problems Series

Overcoming Common Problems Series

Overcoming Common Problems

CONFIDENCE WORKS
Learn to Be Your Own Life Coach

Gladeana McMahon

sheldon PRESS

First published in Great Britain in 2001 by
Sheldon Press, Holy Trinity Church,
Marylebone Road, London NW1 4DU

British Library Cataloguing in Publication Data
A catalogue for this book is available from the British Library

ISBN 0–85969–869–6

Typeset by Deltatype Limited, Birkenhead, Merseyside
Printed in Great Britain by Biddles Ltd
www.biddles.co.uk

Contents

To Mike for his love, support and encouragement

1

Introduction

You've no idea what a poor opinion I have of myself – and how little I deserve it.

W. S. Gilbert, English librettist (1854–1900)

Have you ever felt like you're hitting your head on a brick wall? That whatever you do it's not good enough and that someone somewhere is playing a huge cosmic joke at your expense? If it's any comfort, I've been there and have the T-shirt and CD to prove it. Perhaps that's why I became a therapist – after all, we therapists are all supposed to be angst-ridden! As a fat and spotty teenager I thought my life was over. As a young woman who always seemed to choose the wrong men I was sure losing weight and plastic surgery were my only hope. I did try to do things differently but as I had no idea *what* to do I usually made things worse.

My saving grace was that I was good with people – little old ladies made beelines for me to tell me their woes. Taxi drivers would reveal intimate details about their life and then charge me for the privilege. Friends, family and work colleagues all seemed to think I was on constant tap for information and advice. By 23 I decided I might as well get paid for helping people and won a place on a counselling course. My personal confidence was so low I remember almost not turning up for my selection interview as I was convinced they would not want me. They did, and the next three years of my life became a wonderfully amazing, if sometimes painful, journey of self-discovery.

Now, 23 years later, my life is so far removed from that insecure and unhappy young woman that it's sometimes hard to believe she was ever me. So, what made the difference? The simple truth is that I learnt how to identify my problems and replace my ineffective coping strategies with a new set of life skills. As a therapist and life/business coach I work with many people who feel insecure, inferior, unlikeable and unhappy.

I see clients who are convinced they cannot change because they have been born defective. All my clients are ordinary people who simply want to lead happier lives. They don't all want to be captains of industry but they do want to be able to get up in the morning and look forward to their day. If you are reading this book then it is likely that your life is not all you want it to be.

See if you recognize any characteristics of the people in the following vignettes.

Life coaching skills really do work

Julie

Julie was 31, divorced and had been living in London since she moved from the Midlands when she was 25. A successful personal assistant working for the chief executive of a well-known advertising agency, Julie described her position as one that was 'well paid, with a nice flat, car, a loving family and lots of friends'. At face value, Julie seemed to have the perfect life. However, Julie's personal life was a mess – she always ended up with men who would treat her badly. Her latest boyfriend, John, fell into this category. A short period into the relationship he started to see other women behind Julie's back. Although she had managed to end the relationship on more than one occasion, she found herself constantly drifting back into his arms. Each time she told herself everything would be different, found an excuse to think this would be the case and, each time, she would end up hurt and despairing. It was as if she was on a self-destruct mission. Julie decided she had to do something about her situation and decided to book an appointment to see a 'life coach' – me.

During the following three months we identified a number of problems. Julie appeared socially skilled but often felt anxious and found herself wondering if people really liked her. Although Julie came from a loving family, her father was very strong-willed and had always made her feel as if she fell short of his expectations. She often found it hard to say 'no' to friends and family and then resented the situations she found herself in.

Using life coaching skills and with her active cooperation, I was able to help Julie develop a new understanding about her problem and new skills to change her life. These skills included changing the way she thought about herself and about the situations she encountered. Anxiety management and assertiveness skills helped her deal more realistically with the demands others made of her. She soon came to realize that she was repeating an early pattern of behaviour with John – namely, she was trying to please him, believing that if only she did the right things he would change and all would be well. This was exactly how she had behaved towards her father, always hoping that she would be able to please him and win his admiration. She soon came to see that this was an impossible and fruitless task.

As Julie became more assertive in her relationship with John, she realized she wanted and deserved something which John was unable to offer her – love and respect. This time she ended the relationship for good. About a year following the end of our work together, I received a letter from Julie telling me that she had been dating James for about four months and how well the relationship was developing, how different she was in her expectations and behaviours and how much more confident she felt about herself in general. Two years later I received a photograph of Julie and James on their wedding day.

Mike

Mike, a senior lecturer, came to see me because he was upset about not getting promoted to head of department. He had heard through the grapevine that he was seen as hostile and that this had been a key reason for him not getting the job. Mike saw himself as a hard worker, who did a good job and was always willing to assist anyone who needed his help. He could not make sense of the comments he had received. It soon became clear that Mike did not realize the impact his forceful personality had on others. He was task-focused, believing that doing a good job in itself was enough to gain promotion and the respect of others. He had never realized that people skills were just as important as task skills.

Mike had been in care when he was younger, following the death of both his parents in a road traffic accident when he was nine. His maternal grandmother was too old to look after him and he spent the next seven years being fostered by a range of short-term foster-parents. He soon learned that academic success brought rewards. As he never stayed in one place long enough to make lifelong friends he never learnt the lessons of sustaining relationships and the need for people skills. Using life coaching skills we were able to help Mike explore the impression he made on other people and how he could influence other people's attitudes positively towards him. Social skills, such as using 'open questions' to make 'small talk' and thinking about what other people might want – the 'What do others want?' approach – helped Mike recognize what had been missing from his communication style with others. As he applied these skills, he reported better relationships with his work colleagues and, about six months after the end of his life coaching programme, he gained a position as a head of department at another university.

Jane

Jane had heard about me from a friend who had come to see me because of her anxiety at giving presentations. The minute Jane came into my consultation room it was easy to see her problem – she looked at the floor and not at me, spoke very quietly and seemed much younger than her 28 years. She told me she had been 'born without confidence' and did not know how to manage her life. I asked her what she thought confidence was. Jane replied that it had to be something to do with her personality and was probably a part of her genetic make-up that was missing. I asked her if she would be surprised to learn that confidence simply comprised a set of skills, techniques and attitudes that could be developed – and after some thought she said she was surprised.

Jane had avoided being an active participant in her own life, always believing she would get it wrong if she tried anything new. However, she also envied other people for their ability to get what they wanted. Using life coaching skills, Jane set about learning how to deal with her life more effectively. She learnt that avoidance is based on fear and that when fear is faced in a realistic manner it decreases. What was once frightening becomes normal. Much of Jane's fears came from the things she said to herself in her head – her 'self-talk'. By changing her negative automatic thoughts to realistic ones, Jane found she could take acceptable risks.

Success breeds success, and the more she faced her fears the more in control she felt and the more she achieved in life. In Jane's case much of the life coaching programme focused on changing her thinking style. Three months into the programme Jane gained a place at a local college to study massage – a dream she had always had but one that she thought beyond her. She had also increased her circle of friends and from spending nearly all her time at home she now had an active social life.

Life coaching skills

The three people above all have something in common – a lack of skills and a lack of belief in their own abilities. Life coaching skills enable people to achieve success personally and professionally. These skills fit into four main categories – creating and sustaining positive impressions, developing a healthy thinking style, managing emotions (our own and others) and managing behaviours.

Creating and sustaining positive impressions looks at the way we come across to other people and the range of skills required to influence the best impression possible. Developing a healthy thinking style focuses on how our thoughts shape who we are and how we behave. Managing emotions considers what emotions mean, how to manage our own and other people's and how to use them to best advantage. Managing behaviours is about what we do and how our behaviour helps or hinders us from achieving our life goals.

Life coaching is about developing a life strategy and a way of feeling better about who we are and the world we live in. Life coaching skills are not about finding a quick fix. After all, you wouldn't expect to get fit at the gym without a regular fitness programme. The same goes for confidence-building skills. If you want to get the best from them you need to make a commitment to yourself to practise these skills every day.

Life coaching skills are not a miracle cure for all the ills and disappointments that can come our way. However, people using these skills have found that they can minimize the distress caused by the bad times and increase the rewards and the frequency of the good times. It is a sad fact of life that bad things happen to good people – but many of us make a sad situation worse than it already is by the way we think, feel and behave.

The aim of this book is to give you control over your life, to provide you with the skills to live life to the full. It's always been my belief that 'you are a long time dead', so why not make the most of living? Many people regret not making the most of their life. Imagine how it might feel to wake up in 20, 30, 40 or 50 years' time only to regret all the things you wished you had done.

All the skills and exercises in this book are taken from cognitive psychology, in particular cognitive-behavioural therapy, which is regarded as one of the most effective forms of personal change.

The checklist in Table 1 will help you identify whether you are lacking in confidence.

Table 1: Your confidence checklist

	Yes	No
I like myself.		
I care and look after myself the way I do for other people.		
My life experience has led me to appreciate myself.		
I have a balanced view of my qualities and my limitations.		
I believe I am a good person.		
I do not hold unrealistic expectations of myself.		
I believe that I have as much right as anyone else to have good things in life.		
I motivate myself through kindness and not through criticism.		
I see myself as worthwhile.		

If your answer to any of these questions is 'no' then this book is for you.

Symptoms of poor confidence

People who suffer from a lack of confidence may also experience a range of symptoms and behaviours, as outlined below.

- tiredness
- lack of enthusiasm
- headaches
- guilt
- shame
- stomach upsets
- tension
- significant weight loss or gain
- anger
- anxiety

- poor concentration
- avoiding people and situations
- not speaking up

- a poor opinion of self
- saying 'yes' to everyone all the time
- wishing life was different

If you recognize *three* or more of the above symptoms or behaviours then this book is for you.

How did I get this way?

Many people spend their lives wishing they were different, envying other people or feeling bad about their lack of confidence. Many people believe, like Jane above, that they were born genetically lacking in some way. Confidence is learnt. From the time we are born we receive messages from the outside world and it is these messages that create or drain us of our confidence.

Parental influences

I have never yet met parents who purposely wake up in the morning thinking, 'How can I damage my child today?' Parents usually want to provide the best upbringing they can for their children. However, you cannot give what you do not have. If you think of childhood as a training course, 24 hours a day, 7 days a week, 365 days a year for about 18 years you can imagine that good trainers pass on excellent skills training during this time. If the trainers themselves are not adequately trained there will be gaps in their knowledge and these gaps will be passed on and even the best-trained people can still find themselves facing intolerable life pressures that weaken their ability to offer the love and care that a child may need.

If you were neglected or abused as a child, your view of the world will be coloured by your experiences. You do not need extreme experiences to damage your confidence. If your parents were kind but timid and anxious, or looked after you but were emotionally distant, if they never praised you or seemed to always find fault, then all these factors can lead to a poor self-image.

EXERCISE

Tick the boxes that apply to you in Table 2.

Table 2: My early years

	Yes	No
I felt loved and valued as a child.		
I was happy as a child.		
I was kissed and cuddled as a child.		
I was praised as a child.		

Other people

Apart from our parents, we are also influenced by relationships with other people. Brothers, sisters, aunts, uncles, family, friends and teachers all influence our perception of ourselves. If you find yourself bullied, feel different from your sisters or brothers, have difficulty fitting in with your peers or are cared for by a relative who puts you down, these factors will also affect your confidence.

EXERCISE

Tick the boxes that apply to you in Table 3.

Table 3: My early relations with other people

	Yes	No
I had lots of friends when I was a child.		
I had a good relationship with my brothers and sisters.		
I was not bullied as a child.		
My teachers were kind to me.		

Other factors

Your place in society and external life events such as conflict also play their part. You may have grown up feeling isolated and alienated from other people, for example if your family was poor or lived in a deprived area. You may have experienced harassment because of your colour, religion or ethnic origin. Alternatively, you may have been rejected because of a characteristic such as being large, or small, or having a big nose or some other physical factor that makes you stand out from the group. The following chapters will provide you with the skills you require to improve your confidence.

Now that you have had the opportunity to consider whether you feel you are lacking in life skills, how this lack affects you and how it may have come into being, it is now time to move on. The next chapter introduces you to the first part of the rest of your new life.

2

A Confident Manner

A smile is worth a thousand words.
Anon

Body talk

We go to school to learn reading, writing and arithmetic, yet no one ever teaches us how to read body language. Apart from a very few people who have medical or psychological conditions that make it hard to interpret physical signals, everyone learns the basics of how to read another person's body talk by a process of unconscious modelling. Understanding body talk, or body language as it is often called, is crucial to confident relations with others. As a child, if we made a mistake with our arithmetic a teacher or parent would correct us, showing us what we had to do to get it right next time. If we make a mistake with our body talk no one corrects us. This may mean we develop unhelpful habits that detract from the way we want other people to see us. Understanding body talk allows us to:

- influence the way we come across to other people (both on first meeting and in longer-term relationships);
- understand, respond and deal more effectively with the emotions of others.

You may find this hard to believe, but the words we use are not as important as our body talk in terms of the impression we make when first meeting a person.

EXERCISE

Immediate impressions
Imagine that you are meeting someone for the first time. Allocate a percentage out of 100 to each of the following factors (e.g. body talk 20 + voice 30 + words 50 = 100):

	Per cent
Body talk	___
Voice	___
Words	___
	100

Now look at Figure 1 to see the answer that research into this area has provided.

Are you surprised by the figures quoted? Initial impressions are based more on our body language and our voice than on the words we say. The next time you are on the train or bus, look at the people around you. How are they dressed? How do they sit or stand? What do they do with their hands? What does their facial expression tell you? If they are talking, listen to the tone, pitch and intonation in their voice and ask yourself what this tells you about how they are feeling. Although body talk is vitally important for creating a good first impression it is also important in influencing long-term relationships. In time, many people can tell how a close relative,

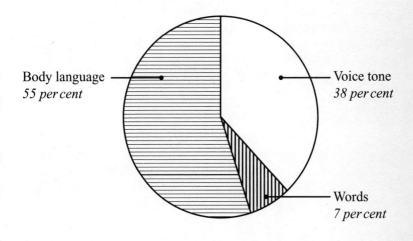

Figure 1

friend or partner is feeling simply by the way they look. How many times has someone told you one thing with their words but their body talk has told you a completely different story – for example a friend may say, 'I'm fine', but their facial expression and general posture looks more like they are worried or sad. You have probably found yourself responding to the way they look rather than to what they have said.

Confident body talk

Eye contact

Cultivate a warm, friendly direct gaze. Our eyes should meet for between 60 and 70 per cent of the time. Any more than this and we are probably staring, making the other person feel uncomfortable; any less and we may be giving the impression of being timid. There are, of course, cultural variations. In some cultures it would be considered immodest or impolite to look a man in the eyes if you were a woman or an older person if you were younger.

If you have difficulty maintaining normal eye contact you can start with a few seconds of eye contact. Look into the other person's eyes, smile and then let your eyes wander over other facial features – nose, hair, etc. After a few moments go back to looking the person in the eye. Alternatively, some people find it helpful to make eye contact and then to move their gaze slightly to the right or left-hand side of the person. This gives the impression of full eye contact to the other person but allows you to avoid some of the discomfort of a direct gaze.

Facial expressions

Match what you are actually saying to the mood of the conversation. There is an old saying about a smile being worth a thousand words, and most people associate a smile with approachability. A smile signals friendliness and a willingness to make human contact. If someone smiles at you make sure you smile back.

Posture

When facing a person, stand squarely in front of them allowing for an appropriate amount of 'personal space' (the amount of space between you and the other person varies from culture to culture). Stand with both feet firmly on the ground, your knees slightly bent and your arms in a relaxed position by your side. Imagine that you have a cord attached to the crown of your head which is being pulled upwards and that your head, neck and back are being gently lengthened. This ensures you stand straight without looking stilted. An open posture encourages others to make contact. If it is appropriate, leaning forward a little indicates that you are interested in what the person has to say and is usually taken as a compliment.

Gestures

Gestures need to match the mood. For example, if you are in a business setting and you meet someone for the first time you will probably shake his or her hand. If you are sitting and someone introduces you informally to a friend you may simply raise your hand, give a slight nod and smile. Some people fidget when they are nervous, they play with their hair or pick bits of imaginary fluff off their jumpers. All this gives the impression of someone disinterested or lacking in confidence. Nodding indicates that you are interested and that you understand what has been said.

EXERCISE

Changing the way you come across

Stand in front of a mirror and practise confident body talk as outlined above. Imagine that you are meeting someone for the first time and consider whether your posture and facial expression would be considered confident and welcoming.

Coming across in a relaxed and controlled manner gives the impression of confidence. When we are anxious or experience strong negative emotions we often tense our muscles and our breathing becomes shallow. If you are feeling nervous or angry you need to make a conscious effort to relax. A deep breath in followed by an out breath helps you slow yourself down and is physically calming. Repeat this two or three times to help you feel more in control of yourself.

Making small talk

When faced with new social situations many people feel anxious and uncomfortable. Very often this is because we believe we do not know what to say and will come across as 'boring and uninteresting'. So many people fear what is often called 'small talk'.

However, many practised conversationalists will tell you that it is possible to have an excellent conversation by getting the other person to do most of the talking. Most people like to talk about themselves and if you ask the right type of questions you can get people to open up.

We looked at the role of body language earlier (see page 10) so – remember – look at the other person, breathe and relax. Now let's think about the type of questions you could ask.

Closed and open questions

There are different types of questions. *Closed questions* are the ones where it is possible to give only a 'yes' or 'no' answer. For example: Did you come by bus? Do you like your job? Would you like a drink? Although closed questions are useful for fact-finding they do not encourage the other person to open up the conversation and you usually have to follow up quite quickly with the next question. Another type of question is what's called an *open question*. Open questions are questions that encourage the other person to talk more freely about himself or herself.

Open questions start with words such as What, Where, How, When and Why. For example: What kind of television programmes do you like? Where did you get that lovely dress from? How long have you known John? When did you first become interested in horror movies? Why would you like to get tickets for that particular show?

In addition to using open questions, many people have found it useful to remember the acronym OPEN as a way of providing a framework to hang their open questions on. OPEN stands for:

Occupation (e.g. job)
Personal relationships (e.g. family, friends, partner)
Environment (e.g. home, work, general environmental issues)
Non-work time (e.g. leisure activities, hobbies, outside interests)

EXERCISE

Using open questions

Think about the following areas of conversation and see how many open questions you can come up with. Remember that the idea is for you to ask as many questions as you can about the other person.

Don't worry if you come up with only one or two in each category. Like everything else, you need to practise and the more you do the more questions will come to mind.

Occupation (e.g. job)

What _____?

Where _____?

How _____?

When _____?

Why _____?

Personal relationships (e.g. family, friends, partner)

What _____?

Where _____?

How _____?

When _____?

Why _____?

Environment (e.g. home, work, general environmental issues)

What _____?

Where _____?

How _____?

When _____?

Why _____?

Non-work time (e.g. leisure activities, hobbies, outside interests)

What _____?

Where _____?

How _____?

When _____?

Why _____?

Risk-taking

You also need to consider the role of *risk-taking* in initiating conversations. Shy people often don't start a conversation with a stranger for fear of rejection and wait passively for someone to approach them. By taking an active role you are the one taking control and learning to be proactive. If you are rejected then don't take it personally. After all, the other person may be busy, tired or upset from something that has happened in his or her life. It may be possible that you have felt rejected in the past and are trying to avoid the same thing happening again. However, everyone gets rejected – that is a fact of life. If you think about it you have little to lose and much to gain by taking an active role.

Listening skills

Good conversation also depends on developing *active listening skills*. Good listening skills help you get to know the person you are speaking to and are also crucial in deepening relationships. You need to learn how to:

- *Listen* to what the other person is saying and feedback the essence of what they are saying. Remember to use your body language to good effect and to use open questions following the OPEN formula for conversation topics. You can use statements such as, 'Let's see if I've understood,' or 'It sounds like you felt pleased about your move.'
- *Evaluate*. Remember what has been said and see if you can make connections. For example: 'You said earlier that you hated flying, but you are going to Spain this year. Does that mean you are going to fly or are you driving?' Does it sound as if the person is happy, sad, enthusiastic or indifferent? Try to use these feelings in your conversation. For example: 'You sound a little apprehensive about your promotion, it must be quite a challenge?'
- *Respond*. A good listener is involved in the conversation and can sometimes anticipate what the speaker is going to say next. Don't complete people's sentences but try and imagine where you think the conversation is going. Don't be frightened to add information of your own. For example: 'I know what you mean about flying – I'm a little scared of it myself, particularly take-off and landing.'

To learn to become proficient at active listening takes time and practice. Active listening means developing your memory and concentration skills and these do get better in time. Try using these skills in as many places and with as many people as possible.

How do others see me?

We are not always the best judge of how we come across to other people. Sometimes we think we are seen as friendly and approachable when other people feel we are too familiar, distant or perhaps arrogant. On other occasions we may believe that people see us as inadequate when they see many personal qualities we are unaware of.

True confidence comes from being able to judge our good qualities honestly as well as those areas we need to work on. To gain a true impression of your strengths and weaknesses you need to consider other people's views.

EXERCISE

Gaining a different perspective

(Don't be afraid to do this exercise. It may dispel some illusions but it will be worthwhile and helpful.)

Choose two friends who care about you and who will provide you with honest answers. Then choose two people you work with who you believe can provide you with feedback and, lastly, choose two family members. Copy the following questions out and ask those concerned to provide you with written answers. Alternatively, choose a time when you are unlikely to be disturbed and discuss the questions more informally.

1 What do you like most about me? List three personal qualities.
2 What aspect of my personality would you most like to change and why?
3 How do you think I come across to new people?
4 What could I do, if anything, to give people a better impression of me?

When you have collected all the answers from those concerned, consider whether there were any surprises. If you are surprised, ask yourself why. Is it possible you have been underselling yourself and not recognizing your personal qualities?

What motivates me?

Motivation is a key to personal confidence. If we know what makes us feel good we are more inclined to take an active role in our lives. What motivates us varies from person to person. Some people need challenges while others need praise. Motivation makes getting up in the morning easier and the more we work on what motivates us the more in control of our lives we feel and the more confident we become.

EXERCISE

Tick the boxes that apply to you in Table 4.

Table 4: What motivates me?

	Yes	No	Sometimes
Money			
Security			
Status			
Achievement			
Power			
Friendship			
Love			
Praise			

Look at the answers you have given and consider how much of what motivates you is in your life at the moment. For example, you may have said that achievement motivates you. If this is the case, how can you go about getting more achievement in your life?

At this stage you may find it useful to undertake a 'life audit'. A life audit helps identify those people and activities that motivate you and increase your confidence or, alternatively, demotivate you and drain you of your confidence.

The life audit

The following exercise will help you identify those areas of your life you would benefit from changing. To gain maximum effect, a life audit should be undertaken on an annual basis, with quarterly 'check-ups' to monitor progress. For those of you who work in a shop or an office you will know all about stocktaking and auditing. A life audit serves exactly the same purpose, as it is a way of working out what you have, are happy with, need to get more of or need to stop doing. Once you have completed the audit itself the next step is to set about changing those areas you have identified as needing attention. There is no point working out what you like or dislike unless you are prepared to change the things you are unhappy about and increase the things you like.

Table 5: Likes and dislikes

Living environment	
Like	*Dislike*
Size of flat	Location – too far from transport
Neighbours	State of repair
	Poor security
	Living on my own
Work/career	
Like	*Dislike*
Environment	Not speaking up at meetings
My colleagues	Lack of confidence when giving presentations

EXERCISE

Write down all the things you like and dislike about each of the following eight areas of your life:

- Living environment (e.g. flat, house, geographical area)
- Family (e.g. family of origin, children)
- Personal relationship(s) (e.g. partner)

- Friends/social life (e.g. friendships, hobbies, outings)
- Work/career (e.g. current job, future aspirations)
- Finances (e.g. budgeting, savings, pensions, investments)
- Health (e.g. diet, exercise, stress management)
- Inner soul/spirit (e.g. your sense of purpose in life)

See Table 5 for an example. Consider each of the things you don't like and ask yourself what you could do to change the situation.

For example, with personal friendships you may decide that you need to become more assertive and ask for more of what you want. As far as work/career goes, you may decide that you need to see your boss to discuss how to improve your chances of promotion and what training might be made available to help with any problems you may have. Research suggests that you are far more likely to carry out your plans if you write them down. See Table 6 for an example.

Table 6: Action plans

Work/career	
Dislike Not speaking up at meet-ings	*Action plan* 1 Enrol on the Public Speaking course at the local college. 2 Need to think about this before I go to the meeting so that I have my comments worked out ahead of time.
Lack of confidence when giving presentations	1 Book a place on the Presenta-tions training course at work. 2 Book a place on the Public Speaking course as this will also help.

Your confidence is *increased* when you take control of your life and *decreased* when you sit back and allow things to happen. You can improve your ability to socialize with others and to create a good impression of yourself personally and professionally. Body talk, making conversation, how others see you and what motivates you all go towards creating a confident you in terms of how you feel and how you come across to other people.

My Confident Manner Action Plan

Nothing will change unless you decide to practise the skills you have learnt, and the following 'action plan' is your opportunity to identify what you need to do and how you will do it.

Think about each of the following questions and complete your Confident Manner Action Plan.

1 Which skills do I already feel competent in using?

_____

_____

_____

_____

2 Which skills have I identified as needing work?

_____

_____

_____

_____

3 Where, how and with whom am I going to practise my confident manner skills?

_____

_____

_____

_____

4 How will I ensure I actually practise these skills? What might get in the way?

_____

_____

_____

_____

5 What date will I put in my diary to check on my progress?

_____

3

Think Your Way To Confidence

It is a capital mistake to theorize before one has data.
Sir Arthur Conan Doyle (1859–1930)

Many people have grown up believing they are not intelligent and this belief has led to a lack of confidence. Society has tended to favour those who are seen as 'academic'. Psychologist Howard Gardner identified seven types of intelligence he called *multiple intelligences*. Current research recognizes the unique contribution each type of intelligence makes. Training bodies now pay tribute to the full range of intelligences by introducing a variety of qualifications for a broader range of activities. A person may have a mixture of intelligences to choose from, being strong in one or two areas and weaker in others. Confident people are able to honour their strengths as well as work on their limitations. They realize that everyone has something to contribute and do not belittle their own abilities.

The seven types of intelligence

Using the scale of 0 to 8 (0 = none, 8 = lots) rate yourself against the following:

Visual/spatial intelligence
You tend to think in pictures and create mental images to help you retain information. You like maps, charts, pictures, videos, movies, constructing, fixing, designing practical objects and have a good sense of direction.

0 1 2 3 4 5 6 7 8

Verbal/linguistic intelligence
You have highly developed auditory skills and are a good speaker. You think in words and your skills include listening, speaking, writing, teaching, using humour, remembering information and convincing someone of your point of view.

0 1 2 3 4 5 6 7 8

23

Logical/mathematical intelligence

You tend to think in logical and numerical patterns, making connections between pieces of information. You ask lots of questions. Your skills include problem solving, classifying and categorizing information, undertaking experiments, questioning and complex mathematical calculations.

0 1 2 3 4 5 6 7 8

Bodily/kinaesthetic intelligence

You have a good sense of balance and eye-hand co-ordination (e.g. ball games). You are able to remember and process information. Your skills include dancing, sports, arts and crafts, acting and using your hands to create or build.

0 1 2 3 4 5 6 7 8

Musical/rhythmic intelligence

You tend to be musical and respond to music either appreciating or criticizing what you hear. Your skills include singing, playing musical instruments, composing music and remembering melodies.

0 1 2 3 4 5 6 7 8

Interpersonal intelligence

You try to see things from other people's point of view in order to understand how they think and feel. Often you are able to sense feelings and intentions. You are a great organizer, and you try to maintain peace and encourage cooperation. Your skills include seeing things from other people's perspectives, listening and understanding other people's moods and feelings, conflict resolution and establishing good relations with other people.

0 1 2 3 4 5 6 7 8

Intrapersonal intelligence

You tend to understand your inner feelings, relationships with others, strengths and weaknesses. Your skills include an awareness of inner feelings, evaluating thinking patterns, reasoning with yourself and understanding your role in relationship to others.

0 1 2 3 4 5 6 7 8

EXERCISE

My intelligence rating

How many of the above types of intelligence did you recognize in yourself? Transfer your ratings to the scale below. When you have done this you can evaluate those areas you have rated yourself highly in and those you have not.

Visual/spatial	0 1 2 3 4 5 6 7 8
Verbal/linguistic	0 1 2 3 4 5 6 7 8
Logical/mathematical	0 1 2 3 4 5 6 7 8
Bodily/kinaesthetic	0 1 2 3 4 5 6 7 8
Musical/rhythmic	0 1 2 3 4 5 6 7 8
Interpersonal	0 1 2 3 4 5 6 7 8
Intrapersonal	0 1 2 3 4 5 6 7 8

Left or right brain?

Our brains weigh about 3lb and consist of about 100 billion cells. Most of these cells are called neurons and, rather like signals in a telephone cable, a variety of chemicals are transmitted between neurons. Our brains generate a small amount of electricity, equivalent to a 60-watt bulb. When it comes to keeping your brain in peak condition, the saying 'use it or lose it' is of primary relevance.

Our brains have two distinct sides, each controlling different types of thinking. Most people have a preference for activities in one side or another. A few lucky people have the ability to use both sides of their brain equally and can dip in and out of either side without any difficulty.

EXERCISE

Which side of your brain do you prefer?

Listed below are a number of statements. In each case decide which statement – (a) or (b) – most closely matches your view of yourself.

1 (a) I prefer logical activities.
  (b) I prefer activities to be spontaneous.

2 (a) I prefer my decisions to be based on a sequence of researched ideas and thoughts.
  (b) I prefer to allow myself to make intuitive decisions.

3 (a) I prefer a rational way of thinking about life.
  (b) I prefer a more holistic way of thinking about life.

4 (a) I would describe myself as an analytical person.
  (b) I would describe myself as someone who sees life as a random set of events.

5 (a) I tend to take more of an objective view of life.
  (b) I tend to take more of a subjective view of life.

6 (a) I tend to break life down into independent parts.
  (b) I tend to look at experiences as a whole rather than in parts.

Mostly (a)

You are a left-brain thinker who prefers activities to be logical, sequential, rational, analytical, objective and broken down into parts. You enjoy logical thinking, analysis and accuracy and you may sometimes be seen as a little aloof by other people.

Mostly (b)

You are a right-brain thinker who prefers activities to be spontaneous where you can take an intuitive, holistic, subjective view that looks at the whole situation rather than simply one aspect. You are likely to be more creative, feelings oriented and like artistic or craft-like activities. You may be seen as a warm person.

No real difference in scores

If there was no real difference in your scores you are 'whole-brained'. Whole-brained people have more options about how to respond to the world around them.

Activities to improve your brain power

Current research suggests it is important to keep using your brain and that those who do are far more likely to lead active lives well into their eighties, nineties and beyond! Whether you have a preference for left- or right-brain activities you can increase your brainpower, whatever your age. There are three ways you can do this.

1 Exercise your brain

Learn something new and set yourself new challenges – join an evening class, sign up for training programmes offered by your employer, surf the Internet for learning sites, read books, take up crosswords and brain-teasers and talk to other people about life, the world, the universe and everything. People seeking to increase their knowledge are not only more interesting but stay alert for longer.

If you prefer right-brain activities try improving your left-brain activity – sign up for a computer or logical thinking course. If you prefer left-brain activities, sign up for a beginner's course in arts, crafts or creative writing.

2 Be more creative

Improve your memory by playing memory games. The following is a great game to play with friends or with children.

- Get a tray and place ten small household items (e.g. key, cork, pen) on it.
- Cover the tray with a tea towel and place it in front of the person.
- Remove the cover for 30 seconds to allow the person to memorize the items.
- Cover the tray again and, without the person seeing, remove two items.
- Show the person the tray and ask them which items have been removed.

Variations on this game include asking the person to remember exactly *where* the items were placed on the tray. Move them around and ask the person to put them back exactly where they were the first time.

3 Watch what you eat

Scientists believe that high-fat diets damage the brain's ability to function. However, diets rich in olive oil may stave off age-related memory loss. Vitamins E, C and B12 and folic acid, together with herbs such as ginkgo biloba, and Korean and Siberian ginseng, have all been linked with healthy brain activity.

Exercise (even gentle exercise) increases oxygen supply to the brain and oxygen increases concentration and attention span.

Look after your brain. Exercise and feed it well and who knows what you might achieve.

Learning styles

Everybody has a preferred learning style. Knowing and understanding yours helps you understand the way in which you learn best. Identifying your learning style enables you to capitalize on your strengths and improve your self-advocacy skills. Learning styles simply reflect the different approaches or ways of learning from which people benefit.

There are three types of learning styles:

1 Visual – learning through seeing
You need to see people's body language and facial expression to fully understand the content of what is being said. You tend to prefer sitting at the front of the classroom. You may think in pictures and learn best from visual displays such as overhead transparencies, videos, flip-charts and handouts. You may prefer to take detailed notes to absorb the information you are trying to learn.

2 Auditory – learning through listening
You learn best through lectures, discussions, talking things through and listening to what others have to say. Auditory learners listen to the tone of voice, pitch, speed and other vocal nuances as a way of making sense of what is being said. Written information may have little meaning until it is heard. These learners often benefit from reading text aloud and using a tape recorder.

3 Tactile/kinaesthetic – learning through doing and touching
You learn best through a hands-on approach, exploring the physical world around you. You may find it hard to sit still for long periods and may become distracted by your need for activity and exploration.

Learning how to change

Whenever you set about learning something new, whether it be a practical skill (such as learning to ride a bike, keyboard skills or using the Internet) or a psychological skill such as changing a behaviour or challenging negative thoughts or beliefs, you go through a set sequence of skill acquisition. This is called Robinson's Four Stages of Learning.

Stage 1 *Unconsciously* *incompetent*	*Stage 2* *Consciously* *incompetent*	*Stage 3* *Consciously* *competent*	*Stage 4* *Unconsciously* *competent*

Stage 1: Unconsciously incompetent

'Don't know it and can't do it.'

You feel unhappy but have no idea why.

Stage 2: Consciously incompetent

'I now notice just how often I have negative thoughts but I don't seem to be able to change anything.'

You are now becoming aware of what is happening but seem unable to do anything about it. This is the awareness stage: for example, realizing you make yourself feel anxious by blowing small events out of all proportion but feeling unable to stop.

Stage 3: Consciously competent

'I now have skills and if I think about what I have to do to handle situations better I can do it.'

You learn a range of strategies that you begin to use but you have to think about what you are doing.

Stage 4: Unconsciously competent

'It was about half an hour later that I realized what I had done and how I could never have behaved like that before.'

Because you kept on practising your new skills your behaviour now seems 'natural'. You are now experiencing what could be called your automatic behaviour – doing things without thinking about them.

Change happens *over time* and it is persistence, practice and the belief in taking one small step at a time that wins the day.

Optimism versus pessimism

The pessimist sees the difficulty in every opportunity; the optimist an opportunity in every difficulty.

Winston Churchill (1874–1965)

Optimists think positively about life, trying to see the good in what is around them while minimizing the bad in the situations they face. Pessimists think that optimists are misguided and optimists think that pessimists are depressing. Some researchers believe that optimism and pessimism are biologically determined through an individual's genetic make-up. However, other researchers believe that it is the environment we are brought up in that dictates the way we think. For example, if your parents were optimists or pessimists how do you think their thinking style affected you?

Research suggests that it is more advantageous to be an optimist. For example, it would appear that optimists live longer, achieve more, and have happier relationships, experience less depression and recover more quickly from physical illness than their pessimistic counterparts.

EXERCISE

Optimistic and pessimistic situations
Name three people you feel optimistic around and state why.

1 _____

2 _____

3 _____

Identify three recent situations where you have felt optimistic and state why.

1 _____

2 _____

3 _____

Name three people you feel pessimistic around and state why.

1 _____

2 _____

3 _____

Identify three recent situations where you have felt pessimistic and state why.

1 _____

2 _____

3 _____

Can you spot any patterns forming? For example, are you optimistic with certain friends but pessimistic with your family? Do you find yourself thinking the worst will happen at work or when you are travelling but feel better around the house?

Pessimism is tiring and drains you of your energy. The good news is that pessimistic thinking can be changed. Changing your thinking style is quite possible if you are prepared to put in time and effort.

EXERCISE

Three ways of improving optimism

1 Make a list of three good things that have happened to you at the end of each day.
2 When you find yourself thinking pessimistically replace your negative thought with a positive thought or image.
3 Make a list of positive affirmations and repeat these to yourself on a daily basis (e.g. 'I deserve more love in my life'; 'I am a happy and successful person').

Another way of thinking about tackling pessimistic and negative thinking is to imagine your thoughts as weights in a set of scales (see Figure 2). On one side go all your negative thoughts and, on the other side, go all your realistic and positive thoughts. If you are a pessimist you are too heavily weighted on the negative side and to balance the scales you need to make an effort to look for the good (increasing the weight of the positive items) while challenging the negative (decreasing the weight of negative items).

Perception is not all it seems to be!

We try to make sense of our world from the moment we are born. We interpret messages and experiences and then make decisions about the world and ourselves from these. There is normally more than one way to view a situation. Most of us are limited from being able to see the whole picture by the way we have interpreted the original messages we receive. The more ways we have to consider (see) the world and the situations we find ourselves in, the more choices we have about the way we behave and the way we can influence other people. We weaken our confidence by seeing a situation from only one perspective.

Look at Figures 3 and 4 and see what strikes you about each one. Perhaps you could make out only one image and could not see the other one, however hard you tried. Perhaps you found that with a little thought and attention you could spot the second picture. This exercise is rather like life. Often we don't see what is right in front of our eyes and, even when it is pointed out, it can be hard to change our viewpoint. Time, patience and a little effort can work wonders.

Self-defeating thinking

There is a simple equation when it comes to self-defeating thinking: *negative thoughts = negative outcomes*. In the first century AD the philosopher Epictetus said, 'People are disturbed not so much by events as by the views that they take of them.' For example, if you stood in front of a group of people holding a half-full glass of wine and asked those in the group to describe what they saw, some would say the glass was 'half full', while others would say it was 'half empty'. The point about this exercise is that those who see the glass as half empty are more likely to be the people whose thinking style causes a lack of confidence. Those who see the glass as half full make the most of what they have, thereby increasing and consolidating confidence.

The ABC model

Aaron Beck, one of the founding fathers of cognitive psychology, has provided a cornerstone to understanding healthy thinking styles. The ABC model that follows describes how situations trigger thoughts, how thoughts then activate feelings and how feelings lead to actions.

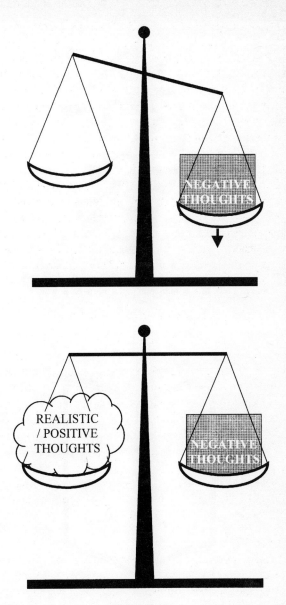

Figure 2

33

Figure 3 Is this a man playing a horn or a woman's face?

Figure 4 Is the book looking towards you or away from you?

A	B	C
Situation	*Thoughts based on beliefs*	*Consequences*
(e.g. standing outside an evening class)	(e.g. I won't be any good and everyone will think I'm silly)	Feelings (e.g. anxiety) leading to actions (e.g. going home without going in)

Negative thoughts

As many of our thoughts are *automatic* we are often not even aware that we are thinking them – they simply seem to 'pop' into our head. In a way it is rather like supermarket music – something in the background that we are not really aware of. Another way of thinking about these thoughts is to recognize the negative nature of them.

Negative automatic thoughts, or NATs for short, are rather like the insects the name suggests. Anyone who has ever been bitten by these little creatures will recognize how annoying these bites can be. Although you do not often see them their bite can irritate for days. These thoughts are usually *distorted*, as they do not match the facts. They are also *involuntary*, which is why it can be difficult to switch them off. We have had many years to perfect our personal thinking styles and they have become habitual and, as with many habits, it can be hard to change them. Anyone who has ever tried to break a habit will appreciate how hard it can be. However much you want to stop, it is easy to find yourself engaging in unwanted behaviour without realizing it.

Types of negative thinking styles

There are many ways in which a person can engage in self-defeating thinking. The most common forms follow. As you read on, consider which of the negative thinking styles you engage in. You may find there are some you relate to very strongly and engage in frequently and others that mean very little to you. It would be unusual for one person to engage in all of these thinking patterns. The first part of the process is for you to begin to recognize the ways you drain your confidence with negative thinking. The section 'Confident thinking' (page 44) considers how you can set about changing your thinking style.

All or nothing thinking

You see things in extreme terms, as good or bad, right or wrong, success or failure. You set impossible tasks and then berate yourself when you do not achieve them. You may not start tasks because you feel you cannot complete them to the standard you want to.

For example:

- You may have set yourself the task of weeding the garden in an evening even though the garden is massive and it is an unrealistic task. However, you refuse to give up and continue even though your back is hurting.
- You may be struggling with a diet and find that you have eaten two chocolates from a box given to you for your birthday. You then say to yourself, 'I might as well finish them all now that I've broken my diet, no point in keeping them.'
- You make a small non-urgent mistake at work and you say to yourself, 'I really made a mess of that, I've really blown it, how stupid of me.'
- You go to one pottery class and find you cannot make anything as well as people who have been going for a year. You decide you are no good and do not return.

EXERCISE

If you decide that all or nothing thinking relates to you, list three situations where you can identify this type of thinking, together with the thoughts that were going through your mind at the time.

Situation   *Thoughts at the time*

1 _____   _____

2 _____   _____

3 _____   _____

Jumping to conclusions

You think you can read someone else's mind, believing you know what they are thinking. This is rather like believing you are telepathic and not checking your assumptions with the person concerned because you 'know' what the answer is. You predict a negative outcome as if you are able to see into the future, and then encourage it to happen by telling yourself it will and engaging in what could be called a 'self-fulfilling prophecy'.

For example:

- You see a friend in the street and he does not acknowledge your presence so you say, 'I must have done something wrong. He must be cross with me, and I had better keep out of his way.' Your friend had just discovered that he had been made redundant and was preoccupied with his thoughts. But you have already decided what has happened and why and have acted on your assumptions.
- You have to give a presentation at work and find yourself thinking about everything that could go wrong. As you do this you feel more and more anxious and then discover that all the things you have told yourself will happen come true!
- Your boyfriend looks at a woman in a very short skirt and you find yourself thinking, 'He would not do that if he thought I was attractive. He must think I am fat.' You don't tell your boyfriend what you are thinking and you sulk.

EXERCISE

If you decide that jumping to conclusions relates to you, list three situations where you can identify this type of thinking, together with the thoughts that were going through your mind at the time.

Situation   *Thoughts at the time*

1 _____   _____

2 _____   _____

3 _____   _____

Mental filter
A mental filter is like having a psychological colander where you filter out everything that's good and focus only on the negative things that have happened.

For example:

- Your boss calls you in for your annual appraisal and tells you many good things about yourself and your work. He mentions one minor change he would like to see in your working practice and you find yourself obsessing about the one negative comment he made while ignoring the rest.
- You would like to join a computer class but remember that a friend once tried to teach you how to use her computer and you found it hard to follow what she said. Although there are many other examples of how quickly you learn, on the basis of this one experience you predict that you will be useless and do not join the class.
- You would love to try for another job at the office and you ask for an interview that your manager is more than pleased to give you. Although your work is valued you find yourself thinking, 'He's probably just giving me the interview to be kind.'

EXERCISE

If you decide that mental filter relates to you, list three situations where you can identify this type of thinking, together with the thoughts that were going through your mind at the time.

Situation   *Thoughts at the time*

1 _____   _____

2 _____   _____

3 _____   _____

Discounting the positive

You make yourself feel unhappy by belittling your achievements and discounting the positive things you have done. When we discount the positive we take the pleasure out of life and this type of thinking can lead to depression, as life can seem pointless.

For example:

- You have studied hard to pass your driving test, but when you have succeeded you think, 'That was nothing, anyone could have done that.'

- You have been dieting and exercising and have lost two stone in weight. Your friends tell you how fabulous you look but you believe you should have lost more weight than you have and feel disappointed at your achievement.
- You have had a busy day trying to catch up on a whole range of household tasks. Although you have managed to get on top of many of the tasks it was impossible to clear them all. However, you tell yourself, 'I've achieved nothing today.'

EXERCISE

If you decide that discounting the positive relates to you, list three situations where you can identify this type of thinking, together with the thoughts that were going through your mind at the time.

Situation	*Thoughts at the time*
1 _____	_____
2 _____	_____
3 _____	_____

Emotional reasoning

You tend to believe that what you feel means something. So if you feel badly you believe it's because you have done something wrong. We tend to make up reasons to match events.

For example:

- You feel anxious about meeting new people and therefore conclude you are inferior to other people.
- You make a mistake and you find yourself thinking, 'I made a mistake, therefore I am a failure.'
- You were a little sharp with a friend and you find yourself thinking, 'I did a bad thing, therefore I am a bad person.'

EXERCISE

If you decide that emotional reasoning relates to you, list three situations where you can identify this type of thinking, together with the thoughts that were going through your mind at the time.

Situation	Thoughts at the time
1 _____	_____
2 _____	_____
3 _____	_____

Labelling

Do you label yourself with attributes such as 'I am a failure', 'I am useless', and 'I am worthless'? Does your 'label' match a core belief you hold about yourself? Every time anything goes wrong, however small, it reinforces the label you have given yourself.

For example:

- You did not do as well as you could have done at school and feel you disappointed your parents. Although you have done well at work you find yourself thinking, 'I am a failure.'
- You are the youngest child in a family of four and your older brothers and sister were good at music, drama and art, none of which you either liked or showed any ability for. Although you all did well at school you always felt that you were less interesting than the others. You find yourself thinking that you are 'pretty useless'.

EXERCISE

If you decide that labelling relates to you, list three situations where you can identify this type of thinking, together with the thoughts that were going through your mind at the time.

Situation	Thoughts at the time
1 _____	_____
2 _____	_____
3 _____	_____

Personalization and blame

You take everything personally and blame yourself even when it isn't your fault. Alternatively, you tend to blame everyone else, ignoring your part.

For example:

- You are due to meet a group of friends to go to the cinema. The time of meeting has changed and you are asked to pick up a friend on the way. However, you did not get the message left on your answering machine as you had already left home. When you arrive at the agreed time you find your friends have been waiting for over half an hour and are cold and a little unhappy. You find yourself thinking, 'It's all my fault, I feel awful.'
- Your boss calls you in to check on the progress of a project. You have had a number of setbacks caused by suppliers not being able to deliver on time. In addition, a number of staff have gone down with a flu virus and this has also delayed matters. Your boss seems very agitated and you find yourself feeling guilty and embarrassed, thinking, 'I am pretty useless. I should have managed to keep us to time and my boss thinks I am useless.'
- You consistently let people down and find that people do not tend to trust your promises. You agree to do a job for a friend at a certain time, on a certain day. You don't turn up until the following day, by which time your friend has completed the task. You find yourself feeling angry and believe, 'He should not have treated me that way.'

EXERCISE

If you decide that personalization and blame relates to you, list three situations where you can identify this type of thinking, together with the thoughts that were going through your mind at the time.

Situation	Thoughts at the time
1 _____	_____
2 _____	_____
3 _____	_____

Overgeneralization

You take one event and act as if it were part of a life-long pattern. You tend to be prone to making global statements about yourself, other people and the world.

For example:

- You are learning a new software package and are finding it hard. You make a mistake and think, 'I always get it wrong!'
- You have just started a new relationship. After your second date you find that your boyfriend/girlfriend has been dating someone else and you think, 'No man/woman is trustworthy.'

EXERCISE

If you decide that overgeneralizing relates to you, list three situations where you can identify this type of thinking, together with the thoughts that were going through your mind at the time.

Situation	*Thoughts at the time*
1 _____	_____
2 _____	_____
3 _____	_____

Shoulds and musts

You fill your life with a barrage of 'shoulds' and 'musts'. You use these as a way of trying to motivate yourself. Sadly, the more you tell yourself you should do something the less likely you are to do it and the worse you feel. You also find yourself critically using shoulds and musts about the way you believe other people should behave.

For example:

- You spend your time believing, 'I should get things right,' 'I must not make a mistake,' 'I have to make people happy.'
- You are having a particularly stressful time and you find yourself thinking, 'I should be able to handle this. I must behave more reasonably. I have got to get a grip.'

EXERCISE

If you decide that shoulds and musts relates to you, list three situations where you can identify this type of thinking together with the thoughts that were going through your mind at the time.

Situation	Thoughts at the time
1 _____	_____
2 _____	_____
3 _____	_____

Catastrophizing

Wherever possible you ensure you make a mountain out of a molehill, gaining maximum emotional distress and drama from the situation. You find yourself using lots of emotional words with dramatic meaning and always see the most awful consequences.

For example:

- Your boss asks you to pop in and see her tomorrow morning. You spend the rest of the day and evening worrying about what you have done wrong and imagining all kinds of awful consequences.
- Your friend said she would pick up some herbs on her way over to your place as you are having a small dinner party. She gets held up and forgets, and you behave as if it is the end of the world and not simply a minor setback.

EXERCISE

If you decide that catastrophizing relates to you, list three situations where you can identify this type of thinking, together with the thoughts that were going through your mind at the time.

Situation	Thoughts at the time
1 _____	_____
2 _____	_____
3 _____	_____

Confident thinking

Confident thinking means learning how to challenge and change your negative thinking. It means learning to replace your self-defeating thinking with realistic thoughts. These thoughts increase your good feelings about yourself and others. Try to imagine that every time you engage in negative thinking it is rather like going to your bank, taking out a handful of hard-earned cash and then walking down the street throwing it in the air. Your psychological energy is just as valuable. It is something you need to invest for a rainy day. Sadly, life has its downs and it is when you face a crisis that you need to be able to call upon your reserves. After all, it's when the roof needs replacing that you are glad you have saved some money and the same principle applies when you face an emotional crisis.

Table 7: Thoughts monitoring form

Situation	Self-defeating thinking	Feelings and actions	Healthy response	New approach
A	B	C	D	E

Table 8: Completed example

Situation	Self-defeating thinking	Feelings and actions	Healthy response	New approach
A	B	C	D	E
My friend asks me to lend her money.	I should lend her the money as she is my friend and she will think I am being mean. *Logical*: Just because she is my friend, how does it logically follow that I have to lend her money? *Empirical*: Where is the evidence that she will think me mean? *Pragmatic*: Where is it getting me holding on to these ideas?	Anxious, inability to concentrate.	*Logical*: Although I would prefer my friend to think well of me, she does not have to and I do not have to lend her any money. *Empirical*: There is no evidence that not lending money makes me mean. *Pragmatic*: Even if she does think ill of me, that reflects badly on my friend rather than on me as friendship is not based on money.	If I change my attitude I may feel a little concerned, but will be behaving in a way that is true to me and respects my thoughts and needs. If my friend takes exception then perhaps we are not as close as I thought and it is better to know that now rather than later. I will be disappointed but I do have other friends.

Monitor your thoughts

As I said earlier, writing things down means you are more likely to stick to your plans. Buy yourself a diary or journal and use this to track your progress. One of the advantages of keeping all your information in one place is that if you have a bad day, where you feel you are slipping back and question your progress, you have an independent record of your success. After all, we all have bad hair days!

The first step in the process of challenging your negative thinking is to learn *how* to challenge your thoughts. Using the list you compiled of your negative thinking styles under the 'Self-defeating thinking' section, complete the thoughts monitoring form (see Table 7), identifying the particular type of unhelpful thinking in which you are engaging.

Challenge your thoughts

Jumping to conclusions

Look for evidence to disprove your thinking. If you believe you 'always get things wrong', think about the times when you 'got things right'. Learn to check out your assumptions and your thinking by asking people what they really think rather than simply acting on your assumptions.

Overgeneralization

Become your own best friend and ask yourself what you would say to someone else in the same position. We are often kinder and more helpful to others than we are to ourselves.

Shoulds and musts

Develop the idea of *preference* versus absolutist statements like 'should', e.g. 'I would strongly prefer to get things right all the time,' instead of 'I must not get things wrong.' There is nothing wrong with wanting to do things well or wanting others to do the things we would like. There is no God-given rule that other people should do what we want, or that just because we want something we should have it!

All or nothing

When you find yourself thinking in extreme terms, look for the middle route. For example, ask yourself if you could tackle the task in stages. Did you achieve some of what you set out to do? If so, give yourself credit for what you *have* done.

Mental filter

Make a point of writing down three good things that have happened each day. Listen carefully for positive comments and when you find yourself obsessing about something someone has said, ask yourself if you are ignoring the positive comments.

Discounting the positive

When you find yourself telling yourself that something you have done doesn't count – stop and give yourself a pat on the back. Make a point of finding someone to speak to out loud about what you have done. For example, 'I am really pleased with my progress at evening class.'

Emotional reasoning/labelling

When you find yourself calling yourself an idiot, stupid, a failure or no good, ask yourself what you *really* mean. After all, what makes someone a failure? You can fail at something but failing at something is exactly that. It does not discount the positive.

The 'Big I, Little I' exercise (Figure 5) can be useful. Draw the outline of a large I – this represents the whole of you – then fill the I in with lots of little I's, representing different parts of your personality. For example, 'I am kind', 'I care', 'I can sing', 'I can cook' and 'I have a good sense of humour'.

Personalization and blame

When you find yourself blaming yourself (or other people) and feel bad because you believe it is your entire fault, draw a 'responsibility pie' (see figure 6). Think about all the aspects of the situation you face and how many factors and/or people have contributed to the outcome. As you carve up the pie you will see that you are only one part of a much bigger network of circumstances. Only take responsibility for what is yours, learn from it for next time, and speak to others about their part.

When you have worked out what actions belong to whom, take responsibility for what is yours and give back the responsibility that belongs to other people. Allocate a percentage out of 100 to each of the people and/or areas you have identified.

Below are some useful questions to ask yourself.

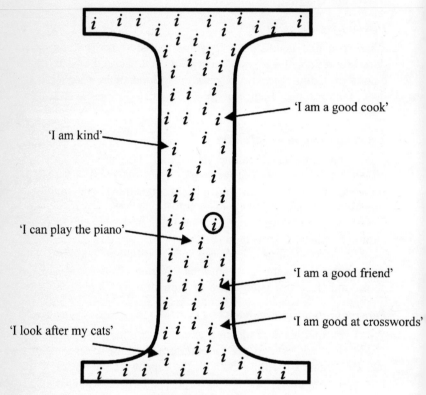

'I am a good cook'

'I am kind'

'I can play the piano'

'I am a good friend'

'I am good at crosswords'

'I look after my cats'

Figure 5 Big I, Little I

What's the situation?

I feel guilty and responsible because my girlfriend was cross with me for not arriving on time at the cinema. I explained that I had got held up in traffic but she still feels I let her down.

What did you try to do?

I tried to ring her but only got her answering machine. I tried her mobile but also got the messaging service. I thought there was a chance she could still be at work but got her voicemail.

What part do you think you played in the situation?

I did stay at work a little longer than I meant to and left in more of a rush than I needed to. *Me = 30 per cent.*

What part did other people or circumstances play?

My girlfriend did change the time and I had to alter a number of my appointments to fit in. She did not check with me personally but left a message on my voicemail. She did not check to see if the change of time was convenient to me. *Girlfriend = 30 per cent.*

There was an unexpected problem with emergency roadworks which slowed the traffic down. *Roadworks = 40 per cent.*

Catastrophizing

Notice the emotive language you are using and tone it down. Remember that things are not awful, a disaster or a nightmare. This does not mean that the situation is not difficult, hard or painful. Use words that put the situation into perspective. Ask yourself, 'What's the worst that can really happen?'

Negative beliefs – your rules for living

Some people hold negative beliefs about themselves as human beings. For example, you may believe you are a failure, worthless, a bad person, stupid, unlovable or unattractive. These basic beliefs act as a constant motivator for your behaviour, shaping your actions in everyday life. These beliefs can be seen as the rules that dictate the way we manage our daily existence.

An example of a life rule would be if you thought you were not good enough and tried to compensate by spending your entire life overachieving or trying to please people. You may live your life

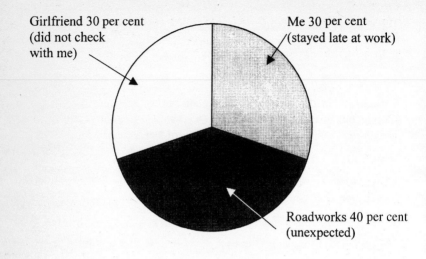

Girlfriend 30 per cent
(did not check
with me)

Me 30 per cent
(stayed late at work)

Roadworks 40 per cent
(unexpected)

Figure 6 Responsibility pie

believing, 'I must always get things right, otherwise I will get nowhere and it will be my fault,' and that criticism from other people means you must have failed: 'As mum does not like what I have done and has criticized me I must be a failure.' You may simply give up on life, be miserable and avoid trying to change your lot because you believe you are incapable of doing so because you are a failure.

People whose life rule is about overachieving tend to feel good only when they *are* achieving. If you believe yourself to be fat, ugly or unattractive you may believe that you are a worthless person because you do not conform to whatever you believe the standard to be.

A person who believes she is worthwhile only when she *achieves* something may find herself losing her confidence if suddenly forced to stop working. Some people believe they are bad people and that if people really knew them, rather than the mask they present to the world, they would be disliked and seen as a fraud. It is helpful to identify your basic beliefs so that you can use the countermeasures described in this book to change the ways you perceive yourself.

Beliefs about yourself, others and the world have been formed by the messages you received from family, friends and the outside world. Over time you have been conditioned to think in a certain way and it takes time to change your belief, regardless of how motivated you are to do so.

Demands that drain your confidence

There are three types of demands we make of ourselves in the form of 'musts'. These are:

- *Demands about self*, e.g. 'I must always get it right' (creates stress, anxiety, shame and guilt).
- *Demands about others*, e.g. 'You must behave well, otherwise it's awful' (creates anger).
- *Demands about the world*, e.g. 'The world should be a fair and just place' (creates self-pity, addictive behaviour and depression).

EXERCISE

Identifying my demands
To help you identify your personal musts and the types of beliefs your musts are based on, write yourself an 'I must otherwise I am' list, as follows.

Demands of self

I must _____ otherwise _____
e.g. *I must be strong and capable, otherwise I am a failure.*

Demands of others

You must _____ otherwise _____
e.g. *You must agree with me, otherwise I am wrong and that would be awful.*

Demands of the world

The world must _____ otherwise _____
e.g. *The world must treat me well if I work hard and do my best, otherwise it's not fair.*

When you have identified the personal demands you make of yourself, others and the world you need to set about challenging these in the same way that you identified your automatic negative thoughts earlier.

EXERCISE

Challenging your demands

You can challenge the demands you are making of yourself in the following ways.

- Consider the impact your demand has on you and those around you.
- Identify how you know when the demand is activated (i.e. the thoughts, feelings and behaviours you experience).
- Think about how the demand came about and the life experiences that sustain it.
- Consider the advantages and disadvantages of holding on to your demand.
- Identify a more appropriate way of rephrasing your demand, which fits with life as it is now.
- Think about how you are going to put your new demand into action.

What if I can't identify a demand but suspect there is one?

Sometimes you find yourself saying things like, 'It would be awful,' or 'That's just not right.' When you make statements like these it doesn't seem at first sight as if there is a core belief in operation. You could find a situation triggers a strong feeling and although you identify your negative automatic thought and challenge it, you still seem to feel unhappy. If this is the case, ask yourself a series of questions and, rather like an archaeological dig, these will help you uncover your core belief. It is sometimes helpful to see your thought at the beginning of a long chain and your core belief at the other end. You have to identify each link in the chain and, as you do so, you get nearer to the end of the chain that holds your core belief.

For example:

    Situation   You are offered an acting promotion by your boss, but you quickly refuse.

Feeling	Anxiety.
Thought	No way, I cannot possibly accept.
1 *Ask yourself*	What would be scary about taking the job?
Answer	There would be far too much to do.
2 *Ask yourself*	Supposing that were true, what would that mean?
Answer	People would look to me.
3 *Ask yourself*	And if they did look at me, what would that mean?
Answer	I would have to meet their demands.
4 *Ask yourself*	And if I didn't?
Answer	People might laugh at me.
5 *Ask yourself*	What would it mean to me if people did laugh at me?
Answer	They would think I was stupid.
6 *Ask yourself*	Suppose they did think I were stupid, then what?
Answer	They would know how dumb I am so I would rather not put myself in that position.
7 *Ask yourself*	So what does it mean to me not to put myself in that position?
Answer	I must not take risks, otherwise people will know I am stupid.

You end up with a core belief, which in this case is, 'I must not take risks and be laughed at, otherwise people will know I am stupid.'

Summary

One way of looking at the role self-defeating thinking plays in shaping your life is to consider the interplay between automatic thoughts, demands/life rules and core beliefs. Core beliefs are the conclusion you draw about yourself as a person as in thinking you are basically bad, worthless or a failure.

Automatic thoughts are triggered by the situations you find yourself in, for example being asked to do something you do not want to do and thinking, 'I should do what Mum wants.' Another way of thinking about demands is to see them as 'if/then' rules, for example, 'If I always please people and do what they want, then they will think well of me.' Core beliefs are absolutist beliefs we hold about ourselves, such as, 'I did not please Mum and she does not think well of me, which means I am a failure.'

A simple way of thinking of this three-stage model is outlined in Figure 7.

Learn to like yourself

The tips on the pages that follow are based on the principles of a therapy called Rational Emotive Behaviour Therapy, or REBT for short. You need to learn to like yourself and to do this you need to accept yourself. They offer practical suggestions and ways to begin the process of self-acceptance. Self-acceptance is the arduous process of learning to like yourself, 'warts and all'. Self-acceptance increases confidence.

Tips to help you like yourself

- Remember that human beings are imperfect, and *that includes you*! There is no such thing as a person who is 100 per cent right, good, capable or strong. If you spend your life believing that

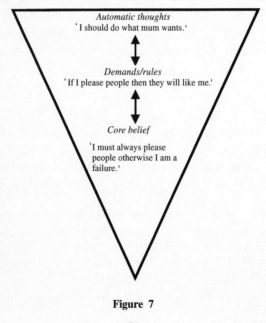

Figure 7

perfection exists you will always be disappointed, unhappy, stressed and in danger of being depressed. There is nothing wrong with wanting to do things well; be a good worker, student, parent, partner or friend. Set yourself realistically high but not impossibly perfectionist standards.

- Develop a belief that everyone is equal, regardless of ability. It is possible for someone to have greater talents or greater skills than you without being a *better person*. Stop comparing yourself to other people, as this can only lead to resentment, frustration or disappointment. If you admire someone for something they have done there is nothing wrong with thinking about the quality they possess or the way they did something, trying to identify the key components so that you can model your behaviour on theirs and learn from what they have done. Modelling yourself is not the same as comparing yourself. There may be differences in what people can do but there is no difference in the basic worth of each human being. One person is not better than another.

- There is no such thing as a 'global rating' on human goodness or badness. No one is ever *all good* or *all bad*. Good people sometimes do bad things and bad people sometimes do good things. If you behave in a way that you later regret, take the appropriate action. For example, apologize, explain and see what you can do to put things right. However, doing something you later regret does not make you a bad person, just as doing one good deed does not make someone a saint. If you keep on seeing yourself and/or others in this all or nothing way you place unrealistic pressure on yourself and on others.

- Overgeneralization (see page 41) is where you exaggerate one aspect of your behaviour (e.g. 'I made a mistake, therefore I am worthless'). If you are hoping to develop confidence, it is important that you do not judge the *whole* of you on just one part of your behaviour. For example, 'I did make a mistake and I am sorry about that, but that does not make me a bad person.' Keep things in proportion. Blowing things out of proportion wastes time and energy. Confident people deal with situations.

- Remember to work on dropping the 'shoulds' and 'musts', as all they do is lead you to develop a conditional outlook on yourself. Dropping shoulds, musts and have tos does not mean abdicating your responsibilities – it simply means stopping putting yourself down.

- Remember that self-acceptance is hard work. It requires energy and commitment and consistent work to make it happen.

You also need to:

- Learn to respect yourself – you are as valuable as everyone else.
- Live a lifestyle that is supportive of your health – there is no point making yourself ill from overwork or abusing your body. If you do this you will diminish your confidence and probably shorten your life.
- Engage in supportive relationships and carry out the life audit described on page 19. Work at your relationships, make sure you have a variety, and cultivate them as you would your garden plants. Tending to friendships pays you back tenfold with the love and concern others will feel and show towards you.
- Set goals for yourself that are specifically designed to improve your life and confidence. When you undertake your annual life audit, set yourself a series of goals for the year. Decide what you want to change and how you will do it. The changes that you make and what you learn about yourself all go towards you developing new life skills and increasing your confidence.
- Recognize that change cannot be achieved overnight and that you will need to keep on working at challenging negative attitudes about yourself. I know this has been said more than once, but that's because it is so important. I have seen too many people damage their progress because they expected too much too quickly and forgot that change takes time.
- Spend time and money on yourself – you are worth it! Learn to pamper yourself. You probably spoil other people, so why not yourself? So many people say they cannot find time for themselves and yet I have usually found that when I sit down with them and force them to find the time they do! It might only be two hours once a week, but it's two hours to yourself.
- Remember that you need to take responsibility for your own life. It is all too easy to blame other people or 'bad luck' for situations. However bad your situation, you *do* have choices. Sometimes it is just too easy to stay in a 'victim role'. Sometimes you have to give yourself what I call a 'therapeutic kick up the backside'. When things go wrong it is helpful to allow yourself to feel your

feelings, to express your emotions appropriately and to seek support from others. It is not helpful to spend time feeling sorry for yourself. There is a major difference between self-pity and self-concern.

Ask yourself if there is a pay-off for continuing to engage in a particular behaviour. For example, if you allow others to make all the decisions for you, the pay-off may be that you never have to face 'being in the wrong', and you can always blame them for the way things have turned out.

Learn to appreciate your good points

If you have been lacking in confidence for a long time you may find it hard to identify and appreciate your good points. Go back to pages 47–8 and complete the 'Big I, little I' exercise, if you have not done so already. If you need more help, ask yourself the following questions.

- What am I able to do?
- What do I like about myself?
- What have I learnt in life?
- How would someone else describe me?

My Confident Thinking Skills Action Plan

Think about each of the following questions and complete your Confident Thinking Skills Action Plan.

1 Which confident thinking skills do I already feel competent in using?

_____

_____

_____

_____

2 Which confident thinking skills have I identified as needing work?

_____

_____
_____

_____

3 Where and how am I going to practise my confident thinking
skills?

_____
_____

_____

4 How will I ensure I actually practise these skills? What might get
in the way?

_____
_____

_____

5 What date will I put in my diary to check on my progress?

_____

4

Confident Feelings

Half our mistakes in life arise from feeling where we ought to think,
and thinking where we ought to feel.

J. Churton Collins (1848–1908)

Become emotionally smart

In the mid-1990s an American psychologist, Daniel Goleman, was
the first person to coin the term *emotional intelligence*. Emotional
intelligence is about being emotionally smart. After all, it is not
always the person with the highest IQ or most qualifications who is
the most successful or happy in life. Emotionally smart people know
how to get the most from their own and other people's emotions.

The skills of emotional smartness fall into five key areas.

1 Identifying your own emotions

Emotionally smart people are able to identify their own emotions.
They are not frightened of telling other people how they feel, and
ensure they take responsibility for their own emotions by starting
sentences with 'I feel . . .' Emotional awareness means learning to
recognize that an emotion is simply a feeling and that feelings are an
integral part of life.

EXERCISE

What do emotions mean to me?

1 Listed below are a series of positive and negative words. Place a
  tick against the words you believe most accurately describe you.
2 Think about the words you have chosen and why you have chosen
  them.
3 What would have to be different to change your negative words
  into positive ones?

Positive	*Negative*
empathic	angry
loving	anxious
happy	jealous
joyful	possessive
caring	remorseful
enthusiastic	envious
warm	resentful

2 Managing emotions

Emotions can be difficult, and emotionally smart people know when to take care of themselves. For example, if I have had a hard day and feel a little low because a special project has not turned out the way I wanted it to, I ring a friend or ask for a cuddle from my partner. I recognize that I feel sad or disappointed and I take care of myself. There are times when you need to take care of the emotions of others and there are times when you need to motivate yourself and others.

EXERCISE

How do I take care of emotions?

List three ways in which you take care of yourself and three ways in which you take care of other people (e.g. take a warm bath, ring a friend, encourage someone to talk).

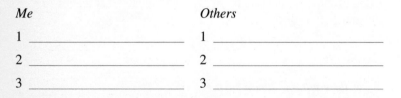

Me   *Others*

1 _____   1 _____

2 _____   2 _____

3 _____   3 _____

3 Other people's emotions

Life is full of people – family and friends, work colleagues, and people we see only once and never again. Emotionally smart people have developed the ability to read other people's emotions. Using skills such as *empathy* (the ability to imagine what it might feel like to see the world from another perspective) a smart person considers how the other person might be feeling, realizing that such recognition can encourage a more cooperative relationship.

EXERCISE

How do I show empathy?

Think about people and situations where you feel empathy. You could choose friends, or use characters from films or television. It is sometimes easier to empathize with fictional characters. Think about why you empathize with the person concerned. Could it be something in your own life that helps you imagine what it might be like to be in the other person's position?

Those I empathize with　　　　　*Reasons I empathize with them*

_____　　_____

_____　　_____

_____　　_____

Now list all the ways in which you would demonstrate empathy to another person (e.g. giving the person my full attention or using certain words).

_____

_____

_____

_____

_____

4　Motivating yourself

Motivation is a key player in getting what you want, and strong emotions can sometimes get in the way. There may be times when it is better to put off your own needs and wants for a future pay-off. Some people find themselves so caught up in their immediate emotions that they forget there is a bigger picture.

EXERCISE

Situations where I have motivated myself and/or others

Think of two situations where you have either motivated yourself or other people. In particular, think of situations where there has been strong emotion. How did you cope with the strong emotion so that you were able to complete the task in hand?

Situation 1

What happened? _____

What I did: _____

Situation 2

What happened? _____

What I did:_____

5 *Effective relationships*

As life is full of relationships it makes sense to realize that some behaviours help cultivate happy and productive relationships while others destroy them.

EXERCISE

Ways of cultivating positive relationships

List six ways to cultivate a relationship (e.g. ringing people regularly, remembering special events or listening to a friend's problems).

1 _____

2 _____

3 _____

4 _____

5 _____

6 _____

Praise yourself and others

If I asked you to make a list of six things that you could do better you would probably have no difficulty. If I asked you to name six things that have gone well recently or that you are pleased with you would probably find this more difficult. The sad reality is that most people neglect the power of legitimate praise – praise motivates.

Some people fear that if they praise themselves or others it will lead to a slacking off in effort or make them big-headed. I have always wondered where this myth started, as it is so far from the truth. It is well documented that children who are constantly criticized are more likely to have poor confidence and to stop trying to improve.

A simple 'thank you', 'you did well there', 'I really liked the way you did that' and 'well done' can work wonders. Success breeds success and every time you or someone else does something well (even partially well) it is one more step towards building confidence.

EXERCISE

Past praise

The last time I praised myself was when _____

_____

_____

_____

The last time I praised someone else was when _____

_____

_____

_____

Future praise

Think of two things that you know you could praise yourself for and complete the following sentences.

I was pleased with myself when I _____

_____

I thought I did well to _____

_____

Now repeat the exercise, but this time thinking about the praise you could give to another person. When you have decided what to say, make a point of actually saying it to the person concerned.

I was pleased with the way you _____

_____

I thought you did well when you _____

_____

EXERCISE

My epitaph

Use the following space to write your own epitaph. How would you like to be remembered?

_____

_____

_____

_____

When you wrote your epitaph what feelings did you find yourself experiencing? Look at what you have written and consider whether you are living your life in a way that is likely to make your words come true. If you need to make changes, what are they and how will you set about making those changes?

Understanding other people's emotions

If you have the ability to read and understand other people's emotions you have a head start in communicating with people and in influencing people's attitudes towards you.

Reading emotions means:

- *Watching body language.* People's body language and voice tone tell you a lot about how they are feeling and your body language is also a way of communicating. Re-read the body language section (see pages 10–13).
- *Listening to the words.* What do the words tell you? Sometimes people tell you what they are feeling (e.g. 'I feel very frustrated').

However, more often people only tell you part of their emotional story – rather like the outline of a picture in a drawing book that you then have to colour in.

- *Using your empathy.* Empathy is the ability to imagine what it might be like to see the world wearing someone else's shoes. For example, someone has worked hard and thought they would be promoted. They then discover their promotion has been put back another year. Although you may never have experienced the same situation you can imagine what it is like to work hard and be disappointed. Empathy can be expressed through statements such as, 'You sound angry about that', 'I imagine you were really scared', and 'I wonder if you felt sad about that'.

How to deal with strong emotions

Strong emotions can be disturbing, both for the person experiencing them and for those around at the time. You may find you are not troubled by strong emotions and simply accept them as part of life. However, many people feel uncomfortable with expressing emotions or being around people who do.

Strong emotions include anger, sadness or severe emotional distress. Sometimes you may be frightened by the strength of the emotion you feel. For example, if you are normally a placid person and one day you lose your temper rather dramatically you may feel completely stunned at the way you behaved. Being around an angry person can be scary, while other people can find crying and being distressed difficult to cope with. You may feel embarrassed that other people have seen you so upset. Those around a distressed person may feel helpless and embarrassed because they do not know what to do.

You are less likely to experience strong emotions that overwhelm you if you make a point of acknowledging your emotions as and when you have them. If you are someone who suppresses your feelings, never admitting them to yourself or others, then these emotions get stored away. One day there is simply too much stored emotion and the natural suppression mechanism stops working and a sudden outpouring takes place.

Alternatively, some people go to the other extreme and believe that they should let all their emotions show all the time. These people lack emotional intelligence as they very often negatively colour people's attitudes towards them by being overly dramatic and emotional.

There are, of course, times when strong emotions are understandable, for example if you had just heard that someone you care about has died or is seriously ill, or if you need to defend yourself against violent attack.

EXERCISE

Identifying strong emotions

Think of the last time you experienced a strong emotion. What had happened? What did you feel? How did you deal with your emotion and what was the outcome? When you have completed the exercise, look at your reactions and ask yourself whether you are happy with what you did. If you are not happy with the outcome, think about what you could have done differently.

What actually happened _____

_____

What I felt at the time _____

_____

What I did at the time _____

_____

Outcome _____

_____

What could I have done differently? _____

_____

_____

_____

_____

Confidence-draining negative emotions

Depression

There are many times in life when we feel 'low' and on these occasions we may use the word 'depressed' to describe what we are feeling. Feeling low in mood is something that usually passes quite quickly. However, some people go on to develop a clinical depression that is likely to worsen over time. Depression can result from extreme psychological and emotional demands and can take the form of a one-off episode following a stressful period or a traumatic event. Depression, in some people, is a recurring illness.

Depression can be triggered by physical problems, such as an underactive thyroid. In addition, excessive alcohol or drug use can be a trigger. Many people use alcohol as a way of increasing their confidence, believing it relaxes them. Sadly, regular heavy drinking to cope with 'nerves' is more likely to cause rather than solve problems. Some people may be genetically predisposed towards depression as there is evidence that depression runs in families.

As some people become depressed over a period of time, they may not realize what is happening to them. Energy levels drop, work performance deteriorates, the person loses the ability to communicate with those around them and experiences a decrease in their 'quality of life'.

Depression and confidence are linked. If we are lacking in confidence we may be prone to depression and if we are depressed we usually lack confidence.

If you are depressed, as opposed to feeling low, it is important to recognize the problem and getting help is the key to getting depression under control. The checklist that follows will help you recognize if you are depressed. If you are depressed, you need to deal with this first or at least alongside working on your confidence.

My depression checklist

If you answer 'yes' to five or more of the symptoms in Table 9 it may indicate that you are depressed. It would be helpful for you to make an appointment to see your doctor and seek professional help.

Table 9: Depression checklist

Symptom	Yes	No
Feeling lost, sad, tearful		
No interest in daily activities		
Weight loss/gain		
Sleeping problems		
Restlessness/muscle twitches		
Tiredness/general fatigue		
Inability to concentrate		
Morbid thoughts of death		
Thoughts about suicide		

Negative thinking

Although some people may have a genetic predisposition towards depression, it is more likely that it is their thinking style that is making them depressed. For example, research indicates a difference in the thinking styles associated with optimists and pessimists. As mentioned earlier, optimists are more likely to have happier lives, more fulfilling relationships, live longer and heal more quickly. Negative thinking styles make depression worse as these thoughts tend to stop people from dealing with their problems.

Do something daily

Depression slows you down and everyday activities seem more of an effort. You are tempted to do nothing, to sit at home and avoid contact. Yet, people who do something daily tend to recover more quickly. This is also true for those who are feeling low and lacking in confidence. The more you engage with the world the more you learn, the more you distract yourself with others, the more likely you are to make friends. Think about times when you have not wanted to go out but have had to, and then found yourself having a good time. For this reason, it is a good idea to design a timetable of the things you intend to do.

Table 10: An example of a weekend timetable

Time	Saturday	Sunday
8 a.m.–9 a.m.	Breakfast and read the papers.	Breakfast and read the papers.
9 a.m.–10 a.m.	Ring Marsha.	Ring Mum and Dad.
10 a.m.–11 a.m.	Visit supermarket.	Walk in the park.
11 a.m.–12 noon	Meet Mary for coffee.	Have coffee and read book in local coffee shop.
12 noon–5 p.m.	Window shopping with Mary.	Lunch with John and Jane.
5 p.m.–7 p.m.	Get ready to go out.	Prepare for work tomorrow.
7 p.m.–12 midnight	Party at Josephine's. Bed around 1 a.m.	Watch TV. Bed around 11.30 p.m.

Doing something helps you feel less tired and encourages you to do more and to think more clearly. Many people find that committing a list of tasks to paper makes carrying out those tasks less difficult, providing a sense of control over what is happening. It is important to get a balance between activities that might be stretching and activities that are easy to cope with. When you feel low you may stop doing things that you previously enjoyed. It is important that your timetable includes some of these activities.

Don't put things off

It can also be helpful to make a list of all the items you have put off. Procrastination tends to compound problems. The more you mean to do but never get around to, the more debits rather than credits you accrue in your confidence bank. If you have a lot of things on your list you cannot do them all at once, so why not rate them in terms of difficulty, for example by using a scale of 0 to 10 (0 = easy, 10 = really hard).

For example:

Arranging assessment at gym	= 3
Completing assignment for college	= 7
Joining computer evening class	= 5

Once you have drawn up this list, start with items that have a rating of between 3 and 7. Anything rated more than a 7 may be too difficult for you at the beginning of the process. Conversely, anything less than a 3 may be too easy.

Record your achievements

Always remember to congratulate yourself on your achievements. Think about what you *have* managed to do rather than what you believe you *should* have been doing. Keeping this kind of a record provides you with evidence of the goals you have set and your success in dealing with these. Everyone has bad days, days when you feel that nothing has been achieved or changed. By keeping these details in your journal you have a written record of the improvements you have made and these help you to realistically evaluate your progress.

Get moving

Apart from exercise being physically healthy it is also good for our psychological and emotional well-being. Research suggests that even mild exercise can have a positive effect. Therefore think about your lifestyle and the exercise you get on a daily basis and whether this could be improved. You do not need to sign on at a gym or feel that you have to play sport. Simply walking a couple of miles briskly each day and walking up and down stairs can do the trick. Exercise not only relieves stress, it also releases naturally produced chemicals which can raise your moods.

Guilt

Guilt drains confidence. We can all do things better with the benefit of hindsight. After all, no one is perfect. We often say that we feel guilty but guilt is not so much a feeling as a thought process. When you say you feel guilty it usually means:

- You have broken one of your value rules, e.g. 'I must always consider other people's feelings ahead of my own.'
- You think only about the outcome of what you believe you have

70

done or not done, e.g. 'I should have known this would have happened.'

These types of guilt are either about the *actions you have taken*, or the *choices you have made*, and the consequences of those choices. A value rule is part of the moral code you live your life by, whereas an outcome is more about what you have done.

There are some people who believe they are guilty simply because they are alive. Someone who feels guilty but cannot tell you why may experience this kind of guilt. This type of guilt stays with the person throughout life unless they change the way they view the world.

Guilt is a confidence drainer as it does not make anything better, whereas emotions such as regret lead to positive action. If you've made a mistake, it makes sense to put it right. People who feel sorry are more likely to try and do something to put the situation right. Those who simply feel guilty are likely to avoid people, places and activities that remind them of the guilt they feel. They may withdraw from social contact and subsequently descend into a depressive state.

Tips for dealing with guilt

- Ask yourself what you feel guilty about.
- Ask yourself, if you were to find yourself in exactly the same situation today, would you behave any differently?
- What core beliefs influence the way you live your life? Is it possible for anyone to live up to all of those core beliefs all of the time?
- Remember the maxim set out earlier in this book: bad things happen to good people and good people sometimes do bad things.
- Examine your 'thinking style' for examples of the kind of self-defeating thoughts described on page 35.
- Remember that you are a fallible human being.
- If there is something you can do to help to ease matters for others, then do so.
- Don't hide away from the world, as this leads only to depression.
- Learn to forgive yourself and remember that forgiveness is a choice that you can choose to exercise on yourself.
- Use the 'Big I, little I' on page 48 to remind yourself of your positive points and use the 'responsibility pie' on page 50 to help you work out who is responsible for what.

Cost-benefit analysis

It can be hard to change your behaviour, particularly if you have been acting in a particular way for months or years. You may not even be certain that you really want to change your behaviour at all, because behaving in a certain way may be bringing certain pay-offs in its wake. A 'cost-benefit analysis' can help you understand the benefits a particular behaviour is playing in your life currently.

Write down the problem you are experiencing, and on the right-hand side of the page list all the benefits of continuing to stay as you are. Then on the left-hand side of the page write down all the costs (emotional, practical, financial, etc.) of continuing as you are.

Table 11: Cost-benefit analysis

Name	Date
Situation	
Cost	Benefit

Table 12: Completed cost-benefit analysis

Name Amy Anyone	*Date* 8/8/01
Situation I almost never speak up for myself.	
Cost	Benefit
• I worry a lot. • Other people make decisions that I don't like. • I feel weak. • I don't get what I want.	• I can't be wrong. • I don't have to stand up for myself. • I can avoid difficult situations.

When you have written out all the costs and benefits of your behaviour you will be in a better position to make decisions about whether you want to remain the same or change. If you decide you want to change you then need to decide how to go about making the changes required.

Anger

A healthy emotion is one that is appropriate to the situation that passes without causing damage either to yourself or anyone else. Anger has a self-protective role to play in our well-being. I am not suggesting you try to suppress this natural reaction totally. It could save your life and individual and collective anger have changed many injustices. That said, there is a world of difference between healthy and unhealthy anger. Unhealthy anger festers and is usually destructive to the individual and/or to those around them and can turn into rage or violent behaviour.

In addition, some research studies suggest there is a strong link between excessive anger and coronary heart disease. Anger is like any other emotion: it has a place, and when used appropriately can produce a sense of energy and determination. Used inappropriately, it damages.

Table 13: Anger checklist

Symptom	Yes	No
Experiencing feeling of anger for no reason		
Acting out your anger on other people		
Fantasizing about taking revenge		
Having dreams or nightmares about revenge		
Hitting objects (e.g. tables, chairs, walls)		
Other people have expressed concern about your anger		
Tension, jaw-clenching		

My anger checklist

If you answer 'Yes' to any of the symptoms in Table 13 you are probably experiencing unhealthy anger and would benefit from seeking professional help.

The likelihood of feeling anger is likely to be increased when you believe you (or the people you love) are not treated well or that you were let down by someone. In many instances, these feelings of anger simply subside in time. Anger drains confidence because like any strong emotion that is not being used wisely it tends to take over.

Tips for dealing with anger

The following is a list of coping strategies, which can be employed if you are unhappy about your anger and wish to gain control of your feelings.

- Use the thinking skills in this book. For example, if your thinking contains too many 'shoulds' and 'musts' about people's behaviour, ask yourself if thinking in this way really helps you.
- Walk away. If you find it hard to control your anger, begin by walking away from the situation, taking time to calm down.
- Use the relaxation techniques outlined on page 78. You may find the breathing exercise the most helpful of all.
- Learn to be more assertive as assertion provides you with an appropriate way to express what you feel.
- Avoid alcohol, as this will exaggerate your feelings even more.
- Avoid drugs (unless prescribed by your doctor). Amphetamines and illegal substances, such as cocaine, will make you feel more angry.
- Plan for any situations you expect are going to be difficult to manage.

If you decide that anger is affecting your confidence you may find it useful to keep what is often called an 'anger diary'. A diary can be used to monitor any behaviour you wish to change and is used as a way of recording the details of:

- when you become angry;
- the triggers for your anger;

- how much anger you feel (using the 0 = no anger to 10 = rageful scale);
- what thoughts were going through your mind at the time and what you did.

Keeping a diary where you make entries at least once a day for three weeks or more can help you identify any patterns to your feelings and behaviours and the types of situations that trigger your anger. The diary also gives you the opportunity to monitor how well you are dealing with your anger.

The role of assertiveness

Assertiveness means asking for what you want while respecting the rights of others. You look for what is called a 'win-win' scenario and take responsibility for your own actions while accepting the choices you have made. Becoming more assertive improves the way you communicate with others. Most colleges and evening institutes are likely to offer short courses on assertiveness. Read Chapter 5 for further information on how to become more assertive.

Shame and humiliation

Feelings of shame can appear in many forms. You may feel shame because you believe you have broken one of your value rules – either a value rule you hold about yourself or one you think others hold. You may feel shame because you believe you have behaved in a way frowned on by society or by specific individuals. Many people whose sexuality does not conform to that of the heterosexual majority sometimes wish they were different and feel (wrongly) ashamed. You may catastrophize about situations, telling yourself that it is 'awful' you feel or behave in such-and-such a way – awfulizing is often expressed in terms of criticism about personal weakness: 'If they saw me lose my temper, that would be awful. What would they think of me?'

People who experience shame have a great capacity for avoiding people and places they believe remind them of their weakness. Another expression of shame is to take the view that 'the best form of defence is attack'. People who adopt this position act out their shame by using attacking behaviour. All of these behaviours are guaranteed to ensure you damage your confidence as they limit the way you feel able to relate to those around you and the activities you are prepared to become involved in.

Feeling humiliated is where you feel you have lost status in some way. People who feel humiliated often experience a strong desire for revenge. They tend to believe that if they could inflict damage on the person they hold responsible for their humiliation they would feel better and that justice would be served. Humiliation is closely linked to the same kind of thought processes aroused by shame and guilt – particularly around the issue of worrying about how others would think less of them as a result of their perceived loss of status.

Tips for dealing with shame and humiliation
Ask yourself:

• Do you really believe someone thinks less of you as a result of something you have done? If so, why?
• Would you think less of someone who had gone through an identical experience to your own?

If you have answered 'no' to both questions, why do you hold yourself responsible when you don't hold others responsible for the same thing?

Anxiety
So many people spend much of their time worrying about life, the universe and everything! Anxiety drains confidence as anxiety is based on fear. It is inevitable that life will not run smoothly and that there will be times when you are worried. For example, if you or a loved one became ill and required further tests it would be quite reasonable for you to have some concern regarding the outcome. The whole area of fear can be rated in terms of mild, moderate or severe feelings. Mild fear could be seen as worry, whereas severe fear could be seen as extreme anxiety. Anxiety disables and it is impossible to maintain or develop confidence while in an anxious state. Any strong emotion, but particularly anxiety, can act as a circuit-breaker in the confidence cycle.

Constructive worry
Did you know?

• 39 per cent of the things you worry about never happen.
• 32 per cent of things you worry about have happened.

- 21 per cent of your worries are over trivialities.
- 9 per cent of your worries relate to important issues where you have legitimate cause for concern.

If you stop worrying completely you would be of little value to yourself, your employer or your family. A certain amount of worry and tension makes you feel better, so keep on worrying. Concentrate on that 9 per cent and put the other 91 per cent behind you.

Your worry notebook

A worry notebook will help you worry constructively. Take any notebook and divide the page into four sections using the headings in Table 14.

Table 14: Worry notebook

Events that might happen	Today's events
1 *Worries for today (things that might happen)*: Sue might be late. Mum might want me to get her pension. I might not have done enough work on my assignment.	3 *Worries for today (insignificant)*: Queuing at supermarket and fear of being sent to another check-out if girl finished her shift before she got to me.
2 *Worries for today (things that have happened)*: Was late getting to work. Forgot meeting.	4 *Worries for today (important)*: Whether John (husband) is to lose job.

Make the entries for headings 1, 2 and 3 before you go to bed. Choose the time of day when you are at your strongest and brightest to complete section 4.

Section 4 deserves special comment. *Worrying about a problem does not solve it – doing something about it does.* Many people fear making a decision as it might be the wrong decision. What people forget is that making no decision is decision-making by default. If you take no action *something* will still happen! I remember working with a young woman who could not decide whether to keep her baby or not and we agreed that if she kept putting off making a decision she would end up with the baby whether she wanted it or not. You need to decide whether you want to be in control (as much as is possible), or if you are going to just let the situation happen. There is *always* a choice, even if the choice is between the lesser of two evils.

Relaxation

When you feel anxious, angry, tense or experience any strong emotion it is useful to do some relaxation exercises. There are many forms of relaxation. Some require physical exertion or movement, while others require nothing more than breathing or visualization techniques. Listed below are a few common relaxation techniques.

The 'rescue remedy' breathing exercise

So many relaxation exercises rely on you being able to take time out, or lie down, or in some way take you away from what you are doing. This simple breathing exercise is one that you can do anywhere, even while holding a conversation, and no one knows you are doing it! It helps to take the edge off your difficult feelings, reduces the negative effects of adrenaline, and helps you maintain your calm.

The rescue remedy in action

- Breathe in through your nose for a count of four.
- Breathe out through your mouth for a count of five.
- As you breathe out, consciously relax your shoulders.

As you breathe in and out, use your stomach muscles to control your breathing. When breathing in use your stomach muscles to push out. When you breathe out use your stomach muscles to push in. This way you breathe more deeply, which helps you gain maximum benefit from this exercise.

Hyperventilation

When we are anxious we breathe shallowly. Shallow breathing means your body gets less oxygen and many people are tempted to compensate by breathing faster. However, breathing too fast can make you feel dizzy or faint. This leads to a condition called hyperventilation.

Hyperventilation means 'over-breathing', something everyone does at some point. For example, when you run to catch a train or do some other kind of physical exertion that requires more oxygen than normal it's essential to breathe faster. However, when you are feeling anxious you may begin to over-breathe and this can prove problematic. If too much oxygen enters the bloodstream it upsets the body's balanced mechanism. Too much oxygen means that carbon dioxide levels are depleted and recent research suggests that it is the loss of carbon dioxide which causes blood vessels to constrict which, in turn, leads to a sense of dizziness. The rescue remedy breathing exercise helps prevent you from hyperventilating. Breathing in a controlled manner is the key to dealing with this unpleasant feeling. Hyperventilation can bring on panic-attack-like symptoms.

This breathing exercise minimizes the effects of hyperventilation. Some people carry a paper bag with them and blow into this when they feel the effects of hyperventilation. As we breathe out we release carbon dioxide so breathing this in again from the bag reduces the levels of oxygen in the bloodstream, reducing the effects of the hyperventilation.

It is important to practise your breathing exercises on a daily basis. There is no point in trying out this exercise once and then waiting until you need it before using it again, as your feelings at the time will get in the way. Practise your breathing exercises throughout the day, get comfortable with them and you will find you incorporate them in your daily life – this is good stress management as much as anything else! If you do this you will really reap the benefits when you need them.

Keep practising the above until you feel confident that you would be able to do it anywhere, any time.

The tense and relax exercise

There are times when you may feel physically stiff and tense and this exercise not only relaxes you but also gently exercises your muscles.

The tense and relax exercise in action
- Lie on the floor or sit comfortably in a chair.
- Tense all the muscles in your feet and then relax them.
- Now tense the muscles in your legs as hard as you can, then relax them.

- Repeat the tensing and relaxing process for each part of your body – hips, stomach, chest, arms, neck and face.

Note: If you suffer from high blood pressure or heart problems consult your doctor before engaging in this particular exercise. It is extremely unlikely but there is a small chance this type of exercise might trigger a setback.

Visualization

In the same way that we talked about people having different learning styles in an earlier chapter, people also respond differently to the variety of relaxation techniques. Some people respond more readily to using their imagination and prefer to use what are called visualization techniques.

The visualization technique in action

- Choose a safe place to sit or lie down.
- Imagine you are in a walled garden at the time of the year you like the most – spend some time looking at the flowers, shrubs, trees and so on.
- You notice an old-fashioned wooden door with a wrought-iron handle on it in one of the garden walls.
- Make your way over and open the door.
- You then find yourself in your own, very special, safe place, a place that no one knows about. It can be anywhere and you can choose to be on your own or have anyone you want with you.
- Enjoy being there.
- Make your way back to the door when you are ready. Leave and shut the door firmly behind you in the knowledge that your special place is always there, whenever you choose to return there.
- Walk around the garden and, when you are ready, open your eyes.

Note: This exercise can take between two minutes and half an hour – depending on how much time you wish to allocate to it.

Anchor yourself

'Anchoring' is where you associate positive, calming, confident feelings to an object. Many people choose a piece of jewellery they wear regularly. However, if you don't wear jewellery you could choose a finger or the back of your hand. In moments of strong negative emotions you touch your chosen object, focusing on the feelings you have linked to it.

Your anchoring exercise in action
- Choose an object – a ring, your finger etc.
- Close your eyes and remember an activity, person or memory that makes you feel happy and relaxed.
- Rub the ring as you think about your happy thought. Continue doing so for five or more minutes.
- Wait for a few minutes and then repeat the process.
- Having anchored your positive feelings to your chosen object, merely touching that object should bring about good feelings.

Using coping imagery to deal with negative emotions

There is research that suggests that when you visualize a positive outcome you are more likely to get one. Coping imagery is used as a way of preparing yourself for difficult situations, for example if you know you are meeting someone or doing something and even the thought of it makes you feel anxious, angry or tense.

EXERCISE

If you do not have a current or future situation that troubles you, think about the last one that did.

For example, Julie avoids people, places and situations she feels uncomfortable (anxious) with or in. She realizes that this is draining her confidence and that she needs to learn to deal with these situations if she is to improve the quality of her life.

- First, write out a 'fears list' of all the people, places and situations you feel uncomfortable with or in. Use the 0–10 scale as a way of rating the degree of discomfort you feel (0 = no discomfort, 10 = maximum discomfort).

Julie's list

Going to parties	= 7
Meeting new people/joining an evening class	= 6
Discussing my promotion prospects with my boss	= 4
Giving presentations	= 9

- Once you have made out your list, choose something that has a rating of no more than 7. (Choosing a higher rating would make it too difficult and choosing a lower rating would not be challenging enough.) After all, you want to succeed and if you make your task too difficult you may set yourself up to fail.

Julie decided to discuss her promotion prospects with her boss as this was rated a 4 on her list – something that would stretch her, but not something that would be overly demanding.

- Now, close your eyes and imagine yourself at the beginning of your task. Use all your senses to imagine the sights, the sounds and the smells. Think about what you would say and what you would do. Think about what you think the other person(s) might say. Use coping strategies like breathing, anchoring and helpful self-talk to help you deal with the event.

Julie imagined herself knocking on her boss's door, asking if it was convenient to speak to her. She imagined her boss saying yes and asking Julie to come in. Julie then imagined herself talking about her job and her desire to progress. In turn she imagined the kinds of things her boss would say and how she would react. Julie practised her 'rescue remedy' breathing exercise, assertiveness skills, body talk and helpful inner dialogue.

- Now practise this visualization two or three times, each time seeing yourself coping with the situation. You may find that practising this exercise actually reduces your original rating even though you are using only your imagination. It is as if your brain is fooled into believing that you really *have done* whatever you set out to do. Once you have practised this exercise a few times the next task is to actually do it!

Julie continued to practise her coping imagery and found that her discomfort rating went down from a 4 to a 2. Julie then decided to do the exercise for real. Although her anxiety increased to a 4 again when she started speaking to her boss, she found it decreased very quickly as she started to use the coping strategies she had practised in her head. The outcome of the meeting was that Julie and her boss planned a training programme for the next six months to increase Julie's knowledge in certain areas. In addition, her boss gave Julie positive feedback about her value to the department that, in turn, boosted Julie's confidence.

Maximum benefit is gained from the above technique when you practise it frequently. When you feel confident enough, follow through with a real-life event using all the coping strategies you have practised in your imagination. Break down your exercises into small manageable steps, as trying to do too much may be counterproductive and could lead to a sense of failure. Success breeds success so make sure you stack the odds in your favour.

If you find it hard to use your imagination, try the following exercise to improve your visualization skills and develop your imagination 'muscles'. Like everything else in life, with practice, your ability will improve.

- Imagine looking at the sky at night.
- Choose one star and watch it become brighter and then dimmer. Do this repeatedly.
- See if you can track the star across the sky.

My Confident Feelings Action Plan

Think about each of the following questions and complete your Confident Feelings Action Plan based on what you have learnt.

1 Which confident feelings do I already feel competent in using?

_____

_____

_____

_____

2 Which confident feelings have I identified as needing work?

_____

_____

_____

_____

3 Where, with whom and how am I going to practise my confident feelings?

_____

_____

_____

_____

4 How will I ensure I actually practise these skills? What might get in the way?

_____

_____

_____

_____

5 What date will I put in my diary to check on my progress?

_____

5

Confident Acts

*If you always do what you've always done, you'll always get what
you always got.*

Weight Watchers

Problem-solving skills

Problems come in all shapes and sizes and you may already be well
equipped to tackle difficult issues. However, some people feel
overwhelmed by the task facing them. You may find that anxiety and
a lack of a structure relating to how to go about solving your
problem stop you. You may find that even if you have a structure for
approaching your problem-solving you experience a lack of techniques in particular areas that hold you back from completing the
process.

Your thinking style, as we saw in Chapter 3, affects how
effectively you manage the situations you face. For many people, a
'problem' is also seen as an opportunity in disguise. Certainly, it can
be a more optimistic way of looking at life and one that carries a lot
of truth. Solving problems provides you with the opportunity of
learning new skills, boosting your confidence and increasing your
creativity. You may also find that problem-solving helps you meet
new people and gives you a sense of achievement.

One problem-solving model (see Figure 8) has six stages.

Stage 1: Identify the problem

Before you set about doing anything to change your situation you
have to identify exactly what is wrong. Just to feel 'unhappy' about
something does not tell you what it is about your situation you are
not happy with and why. When defining a problem it is important to
be as clear and specific as possible about what exactly is troubling
you.

You identify the problem by:

- Writing down what is happening, who is involved and what you
  believe is wrong. For example:

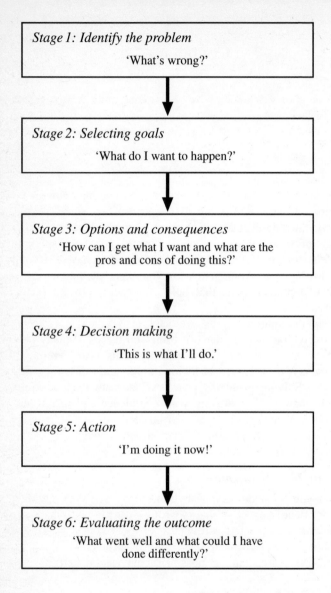

Stage 1: Identify the problem
'What's wrong?'

Stage 2: Selecting goals
'What do I want to happen?'

Stage 3: Options and consequences
'How can I get what I want and what are the pros and cons of doing this?'

Stage 4: Decision making
'This is what I'll do.'

Stage 5: Action
'I'm doing it now!'

Stage 6: Evaluating the outcome
'What went well and what could I have done differently?'

Figure 8 Problem-solving model

Situation: Not able to stick to my diet because I am spending time in hotels during the week.
Those involved: Only me.
What is wrong? I don't seem to be able to control what I eat and find myself eating unhelpful foods and not taking any exercise.

• Drawing a circle in the middle of a page to represent you and then putting all the external and internal influences around you. For example, an *external* influence would be the actual food available, whereas an *internal* influence might be 'my inability to resist sweet foods'.

Stage 2: Selecting goals

Having identified the problem, the next task is to set yourself a goal or series of goals that you are going to tackle. Your goal needs to be specific. Although 'I want to lose some weight' tells you what you want to do, it is not specific enough as it does not tell you how much. A better alternative would be, 'I want to lose 7lbs in weight over the next month.' This example clearly states what you want to do.

If you set yourself a goal you need to have a way of measuring whether you are achieving it or not. In addition to ensuring that goals are specific and measurable they also need to be realistic. Some people have the knack of setting themselves impossibly unrealistic goals, e.g. 'I want to lose half a stone in four days.' If you set yourself unrealistic goals you are likely to become disillusioned, discouraged and feel you have failed. An unrealistic goal is a recipe for disaster.

The next step is to make sure your goal is relevant. It may sound obvious but people often set themselves goals that have no relevance to their stated aim. That's not to say the goal might not be valid but if you are wanting to lose weight there is no point setting a goal about decorating your house. The last part of the goal-setting process is to set yourself a time limit. Are you going to lose 7lbs in a month, two months or six months?

One way of remembering the goal-making process is to remember the acronym SMART.

Specific: Remember to make your goal short and clear, e.g. *I want to lose 7lbs in the next 30 days.*
Measurable: How are you going to measure your progress? e.g. *I will weigh myself once a week on the same day and*

	at the same time each week.
Achievable:	Ensure your goal is realistic, e.g. *If I eat sensibly and take some gentle exercise I only need to lose just under 2lbs a week and this is a realistic target.*
Relevant:	Is this goal relevant to your stated aim? e.g. *Yes, I want to lose weight and I have set myself a relevant goal of losing 7lbs.*
Time:	What time span will you allocate for completing your task? e.g. *One month, 30 days, is the time target, starting tomorrow.*

Stage 3: Options and consequences

Now you have identified the problem and set yourself a goal or a series of goals, you need to consider your options and the associated consequences. When you face a problem it is all too easy to limit your creative thinking about the various ways in which you can tackle your situation.

Brainstorming

Brainstorming is one technique you can use to help you expand your options. Brainstorming involves:

1 Writing down the issue at the top of the page, e.g. *Ways to lose weight.*
2 Giving yourself ten minutes to come up with as many ideas as you can. While writing down your ideas, at this stage do not censor your responses, regardless of how far-fetched you think they are; suspend your judgement; and go for quantity and not quality, e.g. *Stop eating, take my stomach out, spit my food out, eat fruit, join a slimming club, smell foods, have a bodyguard, go to doctors, ask friends, read books, learn more about nutrition, run around a lot, put a tight belt round my stomach, put vinegar on my food, stand on my head, sew my lips together.*
3 Once you have exhausted your responses you can then go back and evaluate your ideas, e.g. *Realistic options: join a slimming club, learn more about nutrition, get a diet book.*

Look for support

Think of who can help you. Perhaps you know someone who has faced a similar situation and come through it – if so, how did they do it? If your problem is work-related, perhaps your organization offers a mentoring scheme you could take advantage of. If your problem is personal you may have a friend or family member who can help.

Consequences

Now that you have identified your options you need to consider the pros and cons attached to each one. As in the cost-benefit analysis (see page 72), it is best to write everything down.

For example:

Option: Learn more about nutrition.

Pros	*Cons*
I will gain an understanding of what vitamins and minerals I need. I will be able to plan meals which are healthy yet filling.	I have to motivate myself.

As well as broadening your options, brainstorming is a good tool for considering the consequences of a particular course of action. In Chapter 4 you were introduced to the power of imagery and using your imagination. You may wish to visualize your options and use your imagination to 'see' what could happen.

Stage 4: Decision-making

By now you will have worked out which plan of action is the best to take. Your plan may require only one course of action or it could require a series of actions, each one building on the other. If you are unable to make a decision it may be because:

- It is impossible to solve this problem and the best you can do is to manage it.
- You may require more information.
- You may be confused about choosing between two or more courses of action.

If you believe the problem is impossible to solve you need to find a way of rewording the problem or breaking it down into smaller sections that are more easily resolved. If you require more information you need to decide where you will get this.

When you are confused between two or more courses of action you may find it useful to talk to a friend and seek a second opinion.

Use the rating scale (0–10) you were introduced to earlier (see pages 69–70) to see if any of the options has the edge over any other. Think about each option and try to visualize how you imagine things would be in six months or a year if you took that course of action.

Another way of working out what may be stopping you from making a decision is to use the thoughts form mentioned earlier (see page 44) to identify any self-defeating thinking that could be at the root of your inability to make a decision.

Table 15: Personal contingency plan
Feeling (rate 0–10)

What could go wrong?	What could you do if this happens?
1 Shop assistant may say no. Rating: 6	1 Use assertiveness skills – three-step model and broken record.
2 I could become anxious. Rating: 7	2 Use my 'rescue remedy' breathing exercise.
3 Assistant may not be authorized to provide refunds. Rating: 5	3 Use assertiveness techniques to find out who is authorized and make my point.
4	4
5	5
6	6

Managing potential setbacks

Although you have considered the pros and cons of a variety of actions you may also find it useful to consider what could be called *contingency planning*. A contingency plan involves thinking about what you would do if a certain reaction occurred. For example, if you wanted to return your shoes to a shop, how many different reactions do you think you could get, and how would you react to each of them? The personal contingency plan in Table 15 is a way of helping you think through and predict all the things that could go wrong and how you would deal with such events if they occurred. Brainstorm as many problems as you can foresee before undertaking this exercise.

You may find that some of your plans of action require practice, for example practising your assertiveness skills. If this is the case you need to practise them *before* you need to use them.

Stage 5: Action

Once you have made your decision you need to ensure you are fully resourced with everything you need to take action. You may find it helpful to keep a note of every action you take, with the outcome. By completing an action plan you can tick off everything you have completed and see how each of your actions adds up to changing your situation. Some people find it helpful to place a series of reminders or post-it notes around the house, office, in a diary and/or on the telephone. These post-it notes act as reminders for the things that need to be done.

For example:

23 November 2001
1 Keeping an eating diary where I am noting down everything I eat or drink. *Completed the diary for today.*
2 A brisk two-mile walk (one mile to and one mile from the office). *Completed.*

Stage 6: Evaluating the outcome

You are the best judge of whether your problem is solved. Using the SMART goal-setting formula (see page 87) makes it easier to measure your success. By making your goal specific it is easier to see how far you have got in achieving what you set out to do. Another way is to use what is called a *continuum*: a line that acts as a graded scale of how far you feel you have managed to come. Once you have drawn your line, place your X at the point that you believe most closely matches your progress.

For example:

Lost no weight_____X_____Lost half a stone in a month

If you have achieved what you set out to do then you can bring the problem-solving process to an end. If you have made no progress at all you need a radical overhaul of the steps you have taken and the decisions you have made. You may, for example, have been rather ambitious in the goal you set yourself. It may have seemed feasible at the time but you may have found the implementation more difficult than you anticipated. If this is the case, you need to go back to the beginning of the problem-solving process and this time break down the tasks into more manageable steps.

You may have identified more deep-rooted problems you feel you cannot tackle on your own and you may require professional help. Where a partial completion of goals has been achieved, you need to consider what went well and what proved difficult. You may feel you are happy enough with what you have achieved or you may feel that you need to take those aspects that you have been less successful with and set about a new problem-solving process with these.

Assertion training

Assertion training encourages people to use skills that build upon inner resources. A person who is lacking in self-confidence usually finds it difficult to be assertive.

The use of inner dialogue is a helpful tool for developing confidence. What you think and say to yourself affects how you feel, and your feelings, in turn, affect your actions.

If you feel confident, you affirm yourself through your thoughts and, in turn, feel even more confident in yourself. Negative self-talk drains confidence.

Assertiveness aids clear communication with other people.

Assertiveness quiz
The questions in Table 16 are designed to help you assess your behaviour patterns. Be honest in your responses and answer each question by ticking the most appropriate answer, choosing the response that most closely matches your behaviour.

Table 16: Assertiveness quiz

	Yes	No	Some-times	Never
Do you say what you feel?				
Do you make decisions easily?				
Are you critical of other people?				
Do you say something if someone pushes in front of you?				
Do you usually have confidence in your own decision-making capacity?				
Do you lose your temper quickly?				
Do you find it hard to say 'No'?				
Do you continue with an argument after the other person has finished?				
When you discover goods are faulty, do you take them back?				
Do you feel shy in social situations?				
Are you able to show your emotions?				
Are you able to ask people for help?				

Note: There are no right or wrong answers to these questions. The answers you give provide you with information about your personal style of behaviour. You will then be in a position to decide whether you are happy with the answers you have given and whether you would like to change the way that you behave.

Four types of behaviour

Non-assertive/passive

Personal feelings

A non-assertive person often feels helpless, powerless, inadequate, frustrated and lacking in confidence.

Behaviours

A passive person does not ask for what they want, or say what they feel. They avoid situations where they have to make decisions. They may act the victim and/or martyr and find it hard to say 'no' to people, which in turn can lead to them becoming over-committed and frustrated. A non-assertive person does not respect his or her own rights as a person.

How others feel

When you are around a non-assertive person you may find yourself feeling frustrated. You could feel sorry for the person at first but then, having tried to help them and in some cases having received no response, you end up feeling irritated and annoyed.

Consequences

Non-assertive people avoid taking responsibility and risks. They want to avoid rejection and the decision-making process.

EXERCISE

Circle the words that best apply to you:

helpless	powerless	inadequate	frustrated
victim	martyr	over-committed	poor confidence

avoids responsibility	does not take risks	avoids rejection

Aggressive

Personal feelings

Aggressive people often feel out of control. Although they may feel superior in the short term they may also feel fearful, insecure, and suffer from a lack of confidence.

Behaviours

Aggressive people shout, bully and use verbal and/or physical force to get their own way. They feel they must 'win' at all costs and anything except getting their own way is 'failure'. They do not respect the rights of other people.

How others feel

Aggressive behaviour can lead you to feel scared, angry, helpless and used.

Consequences

Aggressive people tend to dominate and find that their aggressive behaviour means they do not need to explain, negotiate or listen to others.

However, in the longer term an aggressive person may become isolated and lose the respect of others.

EXERCISE

Circle the words that best apply to you:

shouts	hits objects	bullies others	wags finger
superior	fearful	insecure	poor confidence

Indirectly aggressive/passive-aggressive

Personal feelings

When you behave in a passive-aggressive manner you may feel frustrated, disappointed and lacking in confidence.

Behaviours

Passive-aggressive people behave in unpredictable ways. One day they will agree with you and the next day they will disagree about the same subject. They hold grudges and can bide their time to payback when others are least expecting it. They may engage in behaviours such as sulking and are able to generate a difficult atmosphere around them.

How others feel

When you are around a passive-aggressive person you may find yourself feeling angry, hurt, confused, manipulated and guilty.

Consequences

This type of behaviour is aimed at avoiding direct confrontation and rejection and often leads to a breakdown in relationships.

EXERCISE

Circle the words that best apply to you:

frustrated	disappointed	lacking in confidence	holds grudges
payback	sulking	avoids confrontation	

Assertive

Personal feelings

An assertive person often feels relaxed and confident. Assertiveness does not provide immunity against experiencing difficult emotions and an assertive person has a full range of emotions. However, an assertive person can choose the behaviour they use.

Behaviour

Assertive people ask for what they want, attempt to be clear, listen to the needs of others and respect themselves and other people. They aim for 'win-win' situations and are happy to compromise without seeing compromising as something negative.

How others react

If you are around an assertive person you will usually feel valued, respected, and listened to. An assertive person's behaviour makes people feel safe, secure and fairly treated.

Consequences

Assertive people seize opportunities, develop healthy relationships, and feel genuinely confident.

EXERCISE

Circle the words that best apply to you:

confident	relaxed	listens to others	win-win
seizes opportunities	respects others	respects self	

Assertiveness involves

Respect for self and for others

Assertive people respect themselves and other people equally. They choose to show this respect in the way they openly, honestly and genuinely deal with other people. They will stand up for themselves. Setting boundaries is one way in which we show respect for ourselves. It is up to each individual to decide what boundaries they wish to create.

For example: 'I know that you would like me to work alternate weekends. However, this was not part of our original agreement and while I am prepared to assist with the odd emergency I am not prepared to work weekends on a regular basis.'

Taking personal responsibility for thoughts, feelings and actions

Assertive people are prepared to take responsibility for what they say, for what they feel and for what they do. They realize how important it is to act in a responsible way and that true confidence comes only from honestly recognizing and appropriately dealing with those around them.

For example, 'I feel angry when you shout at me' is more assertive than 'You make me feel angry when you shout at me.' Using the word 'I' is one way of taking responsibility for what you feel, think, say and do – for example, 'I feel uncomfortable about this decision.'

Recognizing and making choices

Assertive people recognize the need to make choices and do not avoid doing so. They believe that even if they make the wrong choice it is not the end of the world. Assertiveness means taking risks and assertive people believe that life is based on acceptable risk-taking.

Three Steps to Assertiveness

Step 1

Using your active listening skills, listen to what the other person is saying and demonstrate you have *heard* and *understood* what they have said. You are more likely to get the outcome you seek if the other person feels you have really heard them. Very often we are more concerned with what we want to say than what the other person has said and this can lead to the pantomime situation of 'Oh yes, you did', 'Oh no, I didn't'.

Jane   I was really mad at you for not helping and leaving all the work to me.

John   I can see that you could have felt mad. (Or, I appreciate you feel cross with me.)

Step 2

In Step 2 you say what you *think* or *feel*. If this stage is to flow smoothly you need to use *link* words such as 'however', or 'on the other hand', or 'alternatively'.

John   However, you did say that you preferred to be in the kitchen on your own and I thought it would be better if I looked after the guests . . .

Step 3

In Step 3 you say what you *want to happen*. To help this section flow from the one before you need to use the link word *and*. You are looking for what could be called a workable compromise, something that will sort the situation out and help both parties learn something useful for the next time such a situation arises.

John   . . . and perhaps we could work out how we manage this kind of situation for next time.

For example:

Step 1	I understand you want all five reports by Monday.
Link word	However
Step 2	I will only be able to complete three by Monday and the remaining two by Wednesday
Link word	and
Step 3	I would appreciate guidance on which three you would like by Monday.

Managing instant reactions

It can be hard to change your style of communicating and, as we discussed in Chapter 3, change takes time. If you find yourself reacting quickly, count to three in your head and take a deep breath. This should slow you down so you can make a more considered response.

Less is more

You may find you over-explain yourself and become long-winded in the answers you give. If this is the case, try to keep what you say short and simple. After all, you can have more than one bite of the apple and do not have to say everything in one go.

Some assertiveness skills

Broken record

There will be times when you have used the three-step model and the other person seems to ignore what you say. In this case you need to repeat what you have said in a consistent way until your message cannot be ignored. The idea is to restate the essence of what you are saying rather than always using the same words. After all, you don't want to sound like a parrot! In addition to melding the broken-record technique with the three-step model you also need to watch your body language. Good eye contact, a clear voice and a confident posture all support your efforts.

For example:

Sue	I appreciate you do not normally provide refunds. However, these shoes are faulty and I would like to speak to someone who can authorize a refund.
Assistant	I'm sorry, madam, but we can only provide a replacement pair.
Sue	I appreciate that is normal policy. However, I bought these shoes in good faith and I do want a refund, not a replacement pair.
Assistant	Well, I'm not sure.
Sue	I can see this is difficult for you. However, I don't want a replacement pair of shoes.

Negative feelings assertion

You need to identify the behaviour that troubles you, explain how it affects you and say what you want to happen. For example, if someone is shouting at you, you may find it hard to listen to what is being said, and you can say so. If the person is sulking you may feel that you cannot get through to him/her to sort out what is wrong, and this damages your feelings towards that person.

For example:

'I feel irritated when you raise your voice (*the behaviour*) and find it really hard to listen to what you have to say (*how it affects you*) and I do want to be able to help you (*what you want to happen*).'

Workable compromise

This works on the basis of finding a solution that both of you can live with. It's about aiming for a 'win-win' situation. It means both of you compromising to come up with a solution. People who aim to communicate in this way increase their bank of goodwill. They see goodwill as a kind of investment that can be called upon later.

For example:

Mum   But you always come over on a Sunday.

June   I know we do, Mum. However, now the children are getting older they want to go out on Sundays. What if we came to you every other Sunday, and you would be more than welcome to come on some of our trips with us.

Mum   I guess that's fair.

Deflecting

Deflecting can be used to defuse aggressive situations. It is based on the principle that no one is perfect and requires you only to agree that the person making the statement has a right to his or her own point of view. If you agree with the person you are not selling out – just simply acknowledging their right to their own view. Most people are waiting for us to disagree with them and all this disagreement gains is a game of 'Oh yes, you did', 'Oh no, I didn't'. If you agree with part of what is being said you can stop the situation from escalating.

For example:

Jake   You always seem to know what's right and never seem to think that other people might have a point. (*This sort of statement could easily lead to a row.*)

Cara   You may have a point. It wouldn't be my intention to come across like that but I guess it's possible that I do. (*By agreeing only to the possibility you act in a way which is non-defensive, defusing a potentially explosive situation.*)

Discrepancy assertion

This skill simply requires you to highlight any inconsistencies in what is being said.

For example:

'On the one hand you say you would like to be more active in decision-making, but on the other you say you purposely keep quiet and I wonder if there is some scope for discussion here.'

Thinking it over time

Changing behaviour takes time. If you have always been someone who says 'yes' without thinking, you may find yourself continuing to do so. One way of breaking the cycle – rather like using a mental circuit-breaker – is to ask for thinking it over time. When asked something, take time to consider your position. If you are on the telephone, suggest that you ring the person back at a certain time: 'I can't speak now, so let me ring you back in ten minutes.'

If you are actually with someone, you can say, 'I need time to think about what you have said.'

I have often found a quick trip to the loo an effective way to buy time. A quick 'excuse me' followed by a few minutes taking time to think about what you want to say can work wonders.

My personal rights

EXERCISE

Consider the following statements and ask yourself whether you agree or disagree with them.

Agree/Disagree

- I have the right to be treated with respect as an equal human being.   _____
- I have the right to ask for what I want.   _____
- I have the right to look after my needs and say 'no'.   _____
- I have the right to express my feelings and thoughts.   _____
- I have the right to ask for time before making a decision.   _____
- I have the right to make my own decisions.   _____
- I have the right to change my mind.   _____
- I have the right to refuse responsibility for other people's problems if I so choose.   _____
- I have the right to choose not to be assertive.   _____

These rights are a way to get you thinking about how you value yourself. Rights do not mean being selfish, thinking only about oneself. Alongside rights are also the responsibilities we have towards others. Assertiveness means respecting self and others equally. You do not have the right to infringe the rights of others and you give yourself the same rights you give other people.

EXERCISE

What other rights do you want to add to those above?

_____

_____

_____

Dealing with difficult situations

Coping with conflict

No one gets through life without having to face conflict situations with friends, family or colleagues. Most people dislike conflict, but many of us make the situation worse by the way we deal with it. Conflict may be part of life but it does not have to be made more difficult.

All of the skills you have learnt throughout this book are relevant to dealing with conflict. The way you think about what is happening will influence how you feel and how you act in a situation. You might feel that people 'should' not treat you a certain way, or you may believe that standing up for yourself is making a fuss. Your belief is, 'I must please people and therefore must not make a fuss.' Neither of these thoughts helps. The first is likely to make you react in an angry and inappropriate manner and the second is likely to stop you from acting in your own best interests. Assertiveness skills provide you with a set of skills to deal with what is said so that you can verbally influence a positive outcome.

In addition to what you have already learnt, there are also some basic rules of dealing with conflict that can be of help.

Work towards a 'win-win' outcome

Try and think about what you want and what you think the other person might want. See if you can give the other person something of what they want, as this is more likely to make them amenable and get you more of what you want with the least hassle. Thinking about what the other person wants is a well-known and tested business strategy. Many people enter business negotiations having considered what the other party's needs might be and how much they are prepared to offer. Very often people actually want less than you are prepared to offer and each point is negotiated on its merits.

Separate yourself and the other person from the issue

When the temperature rises and you want something, emotions can get in the way. Strong emotions block the ability to listen and think – both of which are required if conflict is to be resolved without damaging the relationship. You may not care whether you upset someone at the railway station that you will never see again. However, you may care deeply about damaging the relationship with a friend.

Take responsibility and make clear 'I' statements

Remember that you are responsible for your own thoughts and actions. People do not *make* you think or do anything. It is you that does that. If you want to handle conflict assertively you need to ensure you make clear 'I' statements as a way of demonstrating your needs and wants. Instead of saying, 'You make me angry when you disagree with me,' you need to say, 'I find myself feeling angry when we argue,' or 'I find it hard to argue as I feel got at and then tend to feel angry.'

One issue at a time and know what you want to happen

Your conflict with a person may be about one issue or it may be about many issues. You might find that you have bottled things up and that there is a danger of too many subjects being talked about at the same time. Successful conflict resolution means dealing with one subject at a time. This means making a list of all the things you want to talk about and then deciding which one to discuss first.

The decision may be taken out of your hands as the other person may have approached you. Even if this is the case, it is best to make it clear that although you are willing to discuss all the issues involved, you believe it is best done one at a time. For example, 'I appreciate you want to talk about the way we organize the department. However, you did say that you were keen to resolve the issue regarding your personal flexitime and if we deal with that first we can then move on to the other issue.'

Give undivided attention

If you want the other person to take you seriously and if you want the best possible outcome, remember to look at and listen carefully to the other person. Your basic communication skills, outlined in

Chapter 2, are crucial. You are far more likely to get a positive outcome if you can demonstrate your respect for the other person by the way you deal with them.

Keep track of what's being said

It is very easy in the middle of a fraught situation to lose track of what is being said or to miss the point. You need to check and, if appropriate, clarify what's being said. You can check what is being said by simply repeating the key points. For example, 'It seems you feel I do not listen to you and that you have tried to talk to me many times but felt I changed the subject on you.' This type of checking helps you keep track of what's being said, and restating (in your own words) what the other person has said indicates to them that you have been listening.

In complex situations this type of checking and repeating of the content of what's being said helps you anchor and organize the data you are being given. If you are not sure about something that is being said, ask for clarification. For example, 'I'm not sure if you are angry at me for not listening or because you thought I had not stood up for you.'

The right time and the right place

If you really want to resolve a situation, then think about when and where you are going to deal with it. There is no point trying to discuss something important and potentially explosive if one or other of you is under pressure time-wise. There is also little point trying to resolve conflict if you are likely to be disturbed or in a crowded place. Choose a private location and a time when both of you are free.

Dealing with requests

There are times when people will ask you to do something for them. If you are happy to say 'yes' then fine. However, many people say 'yes' when they really want to say 'no'. There are four steps for dealing with requests.

Step 1: What do you feel?

Many people override their basic 'gut' reaction to a request. Some people not only override it, they don't even notice it. When someone makes a request, you may find yourself feeling uncomfortable in some way. If this is the case, ask yourself what you feel uncomfortable about. It may also help to ask yourself the following questions.

- Do I feel used in some way?
- Do I feel 'I have to', and if so, why?
- What's the worst that could happen if I say 'no'?
- What feeling am I experiencing (anger, fear, embarrassment, etc.)?

Step 2: Saying 'no'

If you want to say 'no', then say so clearly. It is perfectly reasonable to provide an explanation if you believe that to be appropriate, but don't excuse or justify yourself. It can be helpful to acknowledge any feelings you have or that you imagine the other person may feel. For example, 'I have to say no to taking on extra work at the moment as I am hard pressed to meet the commitments I already have,' would be an explanation. However, 'John has asked me to produce a report, Sue is expecting me to reorganize the office, we have problems at home which are taking up my time, my wife feels I am not spending enough time with her and the children and I have to sort out some medical problems,' is more like a justification. There is more information here than is necessary and it sounds like the person feels they have to over-explain. This usually means they feel bad about simply saying 'no' and are trying to justify their position.

Step 3: Saying 'yes'

If you want to say 'yes' then say so clearly. If you are happy to say 'yes' but want to modify what you are prepared to offer, then outline the conditions that apply. For example, 'I can write the report you want but cannot get it ready for Monday. However, I can get it to you by Wednesday morning.'

Step 4: Not sure

If you are unsure about what you want to do, then:

- You may need to ask for more information to help you make your decision.

- You may need to ask for more time to consider your decision. After all, decisions are not always clear-cut, as you may have to decide between the lesser of two evils. In such a case you may have to consider the pros and cons of both before you can reach a decision.
- You may want to suggest a compromise if you believe this is appropriate. This is a way of shaping the request to one that you feel you can meet – a workable compromise.
- Watch out for an 'indirect no' – a way of trying to avoid saying 'no' by stating things in ways that are aimed at getting the other person to take back the request. This type of behaviour means you don't want to do whatever is being asked but don't want to say 'no' either! Don't say 'maybe' if you mean 'no'. Such approaches are unhelpful, as the person will either ask you again (so all you have achieved is delaying dealing with the request) or harbour ill-will towards you for acting in an underhand manner.

Handling criticism

Most people find criticism hard to handle. Many people believe that criticism means they are inadequate in some way or are being unfairly targeted. Although you may not like being criticized and you may not always agree with what has been said, criticism is valuable information that can help you develop personally and professionally. Try to think back to a time when you were fairly criticized. Think about how you felt at the time, how you thought about what was said and how you came to see the wisdom of what was said.

You can handle criticism by:

- Ensuring you are clear about exactly what the criticism is about. This may mean you have to ask for more information. For example, 'You say I am mean and don't contribute enough money towards outings. It would be helpful if you could give me some examples of what you mean.'
- You may need to ask for more time to consider what has been said. After all, it can be difficult to identify what you think or feel immediately.
- Ask for more information if required and then state clearly your need for time to consider what has been said. Wherever possible, tell the person when you will come back to them. For example, 'I

can understand you feel strongly about my contributions or lack of them as you see it. However, although you have given me some examples, I need to think about what you have said and suggest we talk again tomorrow night.'

- Once you have thought about what has been said, you need to decide whether you think the criticism is valid or not. If you agree with what has been said, you need to accept the criticism and discuss any future changes. For example, 'I've thought about what you said yesterday and I can see that I have not been as fair or thoughtful as I thought I had. I think we need to work out a fairer system of contributions.'

- If you disagree with what has been said, then ensure you disagree confidently, making sure you do not apologize. For example, 'I've thought about what you said yesterday and I don't agree. We sat down and agreed the contributions we were both to make and I have lived up to that agreement. It seems to me that you have included items we did not agree together and perhaps we need to talk about these.'

Giving criticism

Giving criticism can be as hard for some people as receiving it. Holding on to negative feelings or simply 'dumping' negative feelings without thought on to another person doesn't help either. If you are a manager you will have to give criticism to your staff at some time or another. If you are a parent you will have to criticize your children from time to time, otherwise they may never learn and could go on to develop unhelpful ways of relating to others.

Criticism does not have to be a dirty word. It is possible to learn from the thoughts and views of others, and if given in the right way criticism can be done in a way that manages to get the point across without insulting the person or being unkind.

Giving criticism effectively

- *Find a private place to have the discussion.* How would you feel if someone criticized you in public? So many people react instantly without thinking about the consequences. If you want someone to think about what you are saying you need to respect his or her feelings. The cinema queue or middle of the office is not the place to talk about any problems you have experienced.
- *See if you can find something good to say about the person's*

behaviour. Acknowledge the person's good points as well as their bad points. The important thing is that you have to be genuine in what you say. Some people try to make up something as a way of placating the other person. This type of false behaviour will be picked up immediately and the person will lose respect for you and for anything you say. There must have been times in your life when someone has said something that appeared positive but you did not believe him or her. An example of this is when someone says, 'Have a good day', but you know they are simply saying it and don't care whether you have a good day or not.

If someone is usually thoughtful or generous or has other qualities it can be helpful to state these. Doing so demonstrates to the other person that although you have something negative to say you also appreciate their good points! For example, 'I have always appreciated the way you have been kind to me. However, there are times when I do feel that you take me for granted.'

- *Try to avoid becoming too personal.* It depends on how well you know the person as to how personal you become in your comments. Keep your comments to the facts of the situation and how you feel.
- *Try not to exaggerate the faults of the person concerned.* It is almost as if some people feel they really have to justify their criticism by making the situation seem worse than it is. For example, 'You are a real nightmare to be around when you won't make decisions.' Other people simply exaggerate because they exaggerate about most things, whether good or bad. Exaggeration does not help anyone. You lose your credibility, the other person feels hurt or unfairly treated and neither of you can win.
- *It is more helpful to criticize the person's behaviour rather than their character.* Behaviour is something you have control over, whereas there may be things about yourself you cannot change, like how tall you are or whether you speak with an accent. When you give criticism you need to ensure you give it in terms the person can understand and can change. For example, 'It would be helpful if you told me when I did something to annoy you, rather than bottling up your feelings and then losing your temper with me over something small.'
- *Describe your feelings and how you are affected by the person's behaviour.* For example, 'I find it very difficult to concentrate on my work when you talk to me all the time.'

- *Make sure you listen to what the other person has to say.* Effective communication requires active participation and active listening.
- *Ensure you are specific about what you want to happen.* For example, 'I would really like it if we could agree a way of talking about what we both find difficult or upsetting about each other when it happens, rather than storing up bad feelings.'
- *The other person needs to understand the consequence of not changing.* If someone knows that a particular behaviour upsets you or damages your relationship, this can be enough to motivate him or her to change. For example, 'If you don't talk to me about how you feel but keep on bottling things up, I will find myself holding back in our relationship and this could end up damaging what we have.'

Managing put-downs

There are a number of different ways in which people may try to put you down. However, they cannot succeed if you don't let them.

There are many types of put-downs and some of these are listed below.

Making decisions for you

Trying to make a decision for you puts you down as it takes away your personal responsibility. It is as if someone knows better than you do what is right and wrong for you. Very often people think they know best and take control of the situation. If this is the case, you need to let the person know that you are capable of making your own decisions. For example, 'I appreciate you are only trying to help. However, I want to sort this situation out myself.'

Putting pressure on you

Sometimes people drop something on us when we are least expecting it as a way of trying to force us to make a decision or go along with what they are saying. This type of action puts you on the spot. If this is the case, you need to ask for time to think about what's being asked of you.

Labelling you

You may find that people try to label you with terms such as 'stupid', 'idiot' or 'ridiculous'. If this is the case, you need to clearly explain why it isn't true and that it is unacceptable to call you names. For example, 'Although I misunderstood what you said, that does not mean I am ridiculous.'

Stereotyping

Someone may try to stereotype you with comments like, 'All women are . . .', or 'What do you expect from a man?' If this is the case, then you need to let the person know that you are an individual. For example, 'I'm talking about how I feel and that has nothing to do with how other women choose to react.'

Making claims that you are lying

A person may suggest directly or indirectly that what you have said is not true, the inference being that you are lying. If this is the case, you need to be clear about what you are saying. For example, 'It is my understanding that Jane was the last person to leave the office.'

Additional ways of coping with put-downs

- Clearly say that you believe the other person is putting you down.
- If you are not sure what is going on, then ask for more information and see if you can find out whether the other person has a 'hidden agenda'.
- Be clear about what you want to happen.
- Remember to use your assertiveness skills.

My Confident Acts Action Plan

Think about each of the following questions and complete your Confident Acts Action Plan based on what you have learnt.

1 Which confident acts do I already feel competent in using?

_____

_____

_____

_____

2 Which confident acts have I identified as needing work?

_____

_____

_____

_____

3 Where, with whom and how am I going to practise my confident acts?

_____

_____

_____

_____

4 How will I ensure I actually practise these skills? What might get in the way?

_____

_____

_____

_____

5 What date will I put in my diary to check on my progress?

_____

6
A Confident Life Requires . . .

You now have the skills to improve the way you interact with other people, influencing a more positive outcome for yourself. Although you have the personal skills there are still some common areas of concern that you need to consider before you can really say you live a confident life.

Time management

Everyone needs to know how to manage time. If you are unable to manage your time effectively you will not follow through on the promises you make yourself to improve your life. You might find yourself wanting and wishing things to be different but saying you don't have enough time to practise your new skills. If you don't practise, nothing is likely to change. There are many conflicting demands on your time, such as balancing work, day-to-day activities, home and social life.

Time is a valuable commodity. How many times do you catch yourself saying, 'I want to but don't have the time,' or 'There really does seem too much to do.' Too much activity leads to exhaustion; too little and you could become bored and frustrated. There are 168 hours in a week and 8,736 hours in a 365-day year, so with a finite amount of time it is important that you make the most of what you have.

EXERCISE

To help you consider your time management needs, think about the activities in which you are involved on a weekly basis and list these in Table 17.

Table 17: Weekly time allocation

Activity e.g. Family commitments, Travel	Time allocation

Allocating your time effectively

Ask yourself the following questions:

1 Do I have time to do what I would like to?   Yes/No
2 Do I put off activities because I have too much to do? Yes/No
3 Do I feel there simply is not enough time?   Yes/No
4 Have I ever thought about the way I use my time?   Yes/No
5 Am I happy about the way I allocate my time?   Yes/No

If you have answered 'yes' to 2 and 3 and 'no' to 1, 4 and 5 you might need to consider how you allocate your time and whether this is effective for you.

Time allocation pie

Time can be divided into six areas and it may be helpful to draw a circle, labelling this your 'time allocation pie'. Consider each of the six areas below and divide your pie into the portions that you believe

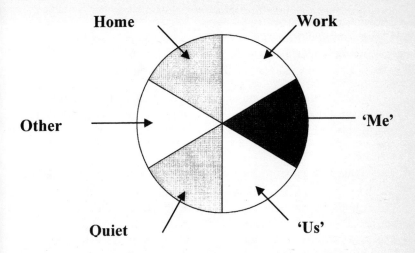

Figure 9 Time allocation pie

accurately represents your allocation of time over a one-week period.

Work time	Time earmarked for work, paid or voluntary.
Home time	Time for housework/maintenance, personal care and gardening.
Other time	Time for family, friends and children.
'Me' time	Time for hobbies, relaxation, exercise and sleep.
'Us' time	Time to spend with our partner.
Quiet time	Time to ourselves for thinking, evaluating and reflecting (e.g. how well you are doing at your learning to be your own life coach).

If you are not happy with the amount of time you have allocated to any activity, consider how your time could be reallocated so that you achieve the balance you are seeking. If there are slices of your pie that are greatly out of balance you may find it helpful to keep a written record of your feelings about how you have allocated your time over the one-week period.

Apart from completing the time allocation pie you could also consider:

- How you manage your time.
- How you fritter your time away.
- How you could be more effective in managing your time.
- How you could make more time to do the things you like.
- How you could do less of the things you dislike.

At the end of the week you should have a better idea of how you spend your time and for what things you would like to create more or less time.

Prime time

Your biological clock has an effect on time management, as there will be parts of the day when you will feel more alert than others. For example, some people prefer mornings, feeling full of energy, but find they feel exhausted by mid-afternoon. If this is the case, it makes sense to try, wherever possible, to save your difficult tasks for the time of the day when you have most energy. Your best time of day is often called your *prime time*.

Using your emotional intelligence to consider other people's prime time can also be helpful, as there may be particular times of the day when it would be best to approach certain people. After all, if there are times of the day when you are more energetic and amenable, why not seek out such times in others as this may help influence a positive outcome.

Methods of time management

There are three methods of time management to consider:

1 Use checklists and notes as ways of keeping track of the work you have to do.
2 Use calendars and appointment books for planning ahead.
3 Focus on short, medium and long-term goal-setting and the recognition of your personal values and desires.

Poor organization

Poor organization can come in many forms.

- A poorly maintained filing system (e.g. filing not done on a regular basis). Valuable time can be lost looking for information.
- No system to identify relevant information (e.g. papers and documentation simply thrown into a pile).

116

- Indiscriminately keeping everything that is sent, filling valuable space, as well as using time to locate items – the 'just in case' principle.

Recently a colleague of mine whose office had become more like a European 'paper-mountain' found it a useful, if difficult, experience to allow his partner to take charge of 'de-cluttering' his office. This exercise led to the filling of 40 large black sacks of non-sensitive information! While getting rid of non-essential items saves time, this only works if an appropriate system is then put in place which inhibits the same problem from occurring again. For example, become ruthless at throwing out junk mail and make a point of filing paperwork on a regular basis.

Non-productive social contact

From a stress management point of view, regular social contact is crucial. However, if you find yourself spending more time than is feasible in non-productive discussions either at work or with friends when you need to be doing something else, you need to consider the following:

- Keep conversations short.
- Keep a clock nearby to remind you to deal with a telephone call effectively.
- Learn how to use the three-step model of assertiveness.
  Step 1   I understand your problem.
              e.g. *I do appreciate your need to speak to me.*
  Step 2   However, I think or feel . . .
              e.g. *However, I need to complete my report now . . .*
  Step 3   and I suggest . . .
              e.g. *and I suggest we speak at 10 a.m. when I can give you my full attention.*

Time management systems

A very basic time management system may comprise some or all of the following:

Diaries, personal and electronic organizers

Diaries and personal or electronic organizers are mechanisms for keeping track of appointments and planning ahead. If you use a diary or personal organizer you may also find it useful to mark your appointments in pencil as this allows for appointments to be changed with the minimum of fuss. If you choose to use an electronic organizer you need to ensure that the data is backed-up on a regular basis to protect against loss of information.

If you use a computer or electronic organizer, the more frequently information is backed-up the less disruption is likely to take place should an accident happen and data be lost. It can also be wise to back-up mechanical systems such as personal organizers as loss of data from these can also cause considerable distress and disorientation. For example, keep two address books, one being a back-up copy, updated regularly.

To-do lists

A *to-do list* is a form of memory jogger. In addition to recording tasks to be done, a simple system of categorization such as the A, B, C one below can be used as a way of organizing priorities.

A = *Urgent items* which require immediate attention, e.g. telephone calls to be made, reports to be written, information required by a certain time of day.

B = *Important items* which require attention in the near future, e.g. booking a holiday, getting a new outfit for a wedding.

C = *Non-essential or non-urgent items*, e.g. details of a new restaurant or evening classes to start later in the year.

Post-it notes

Some people find it helpful to place post-it notes in full view to remind them to carry out urgent tasks. This may prove particularly effective for those who are working on improving their time management and, in particular, setting priorities.

Filing systems

A portable lockable filing system can prove useful to help you store all household and other important documentation. Being able to find something straightaway can really save you time.

Summary

Time management is as much about attitude and organization as it is about diaries and finding information. Effective time management means thinking about what you do, how you do it and how you can make the most of this finite resource. After all, unlike most items, time cannot be stored for future use.

To ensure that you use your time effectively you need to build in 'quiet' time as outlined above as a legitimate activity. In business, senior people will take time out of a busy work schedule to think about what they are doing. This type of activity enables you to evaluate the present while considering the future.

My Time Management Action Plan

Think about each of the following questions and complete your Time Management Action Plan based on the activities in this section.

1 Which time management techniques do I already feel competent in using?

_____

_____

_____

_____

2 Which time management techniques have I identified as needing work?

_____

_____

_____

_____

3 How will I ensure I actually practise these skills? What might get in the way?

_____

_____

_____

4 What date will I put in my diary to check on my progress?

Stress Busting

Stress involves a complex relationship between the demands made on a person and the personal and external resources he or she has to meet these demands.

The demands that are made of you could be 'internal', i.e. your own thinking style. Perfectionists put pressure on themselves and this is therefore an internal demand, as no one else is making it. Your resources comprise factors such as your physical health, financial security, and social and family support. Keep a balance so that you do not have more demands than you have resources to deal with them. If demands exceed resources, you may feel you cannot cope and this is the beginning of what has become known as stress.

Some people talk about healthy and unhealthy stress, meaning that some stress is good for you. I have always believed that it is easier to think in terms of *pressure* and *stress*. Pressure is healthy and something that can motivate you. Some people love to live in a pressurized way, with lots of deadlines and things to do. The distinction between pressure and stress is that when you experience pressure you have the resources you need to deal with the demands being made of you. Pressure turns to stress when the pressure becomes too great, lasts too long, comes suddenly and ends up with you feeling it cannot be controlled.

Stress is a very personal matter. A situation that might stress your friend may not affect you, and vice versa. An event may have proved stressful to you at one point in your life but you may have developed additional resources to deal with the situation as you have grown older.

Work can be a great source of stress – time pressures, excessive workload, poor relations with colleagues/managers, poor communications within your organization, exposure to continual change, lack of training to do the job and job insecurity all play their part. Stress can be experienced in your personal life – family problems, life changes/crises, increasing demands between home and work may all affect us.

Symptoms of stress

People who suffer from stress can experience a variety of symptoms that fall into four broad categories: physical (your body's response), emotional (what you feel), behavioural (the things you do) and personal thinking style (the way you think).

The following are some of the most common signs and symptoms to look out for.

Physical signs
- tightness in chest
- chest pain and/or palpitations
- indigestion
- breathlessness
- nausea
- muscle twitches
- aches and pains
- headaches
- skin conditions
- recurrence of previous illnesses/allergies
- constipation/diarrhoea
- weight loss or weight gain
- change in menstrual cycle for women
- tiredness

Emotional signs
- mood swings
- feeling anxious
- feeling tense
- feeling angry
- feeling guilty
- feelings of shame
- having no enthusiasm
- becoming more cynical
- feeling out of control
- feeling helpless
- decrease in confidence/self-esteem
- poor concentration

Behavioural signs

- drop in work performance
- more inclined to become accident prone
- drinking and smoking more
- overeating/loss of appetite
- change in sleeping patterns
- poor time management
- too busy to relax
- withdrawing from family and friends
- loss of interest in sex
- poor judgement
- inability to express feelings
- over-reacting

Personal thoughts

- 'I am a failure.'
- 'I should be able to cope.'
- 'Why is everyone getting at me?'
- 'No one understands.'
- 'I don't know what to do.'
- 'I can't cope.'
- loss of judgement

How we respond to stress

Our bodies are biologically programmed with what is called the 'stress response'. Most people know this as 'flight or fight'. When you perceive danger your body prepares for action. Stress hormones such as adrenaline, noradrenaline and cortisol are released into the bloodstream, together with fatty acids and sugars.

Adrenaline is normally associated with the 'flight' part of the response, noradrenaline with the 'fight' part of the response, while cortisol acts as the 'on/off' switch. Although it is important to be able to call upon the stress response in times of need it is also important to be able to switch it off.

The stress response is meant to help you deal with demanding life events. However, if you live in a constant state of biological readiness the immune system becomes weakened. Depression and nervous breakdown may result from such prolonged exposure.

The good news is that the progress of stress can be seen rather like a train journey. You can get on the wrong train, and the sooner you recognize the fact and get off, the smaller the distance to return to your starting point. Sadly, some people fail to recognize their limitations, while for others the external demands are so prolonged and excessive that the train journey continues all the way to the end of the line.

In summary, the stress response is important to the survival of human beings. But as with so many things in life, too much of a good thing can become harmful. Stress drains people of their confidence.

Stressful life events

In 1967, Thomas Holmes and Richard Rahe, two American psychologists, published a scale of 43 life events considered to be stressful. Each event was scored according to the degree of stress associated with the activity. Listed below are the top seven items, together with the score associated with each event.

Life event	Score
Death of a partner	100
Divorce	73
Marital separation	65
Imprisonment	63
Death of a close family member	63
Personal illness or injury	53
Marriage	50

In addition to the above, other items included:

- dealing with Christmas
- pregnancy
- sexual difficulties
- legal action
- moving house
- changing school or college
- change in living conditions
- change in hours or working conditions
- arguments with partners or family
- adoption or birth of a child.

One of the advantages of understanding the impact of life events is that it can help you anticipate stressful events. For example, knowing that having a baby can be stressful allows you to consider what stress management techniques are likely to help you. A fact that surprises many people is that life events seen as pleasurable also carry a stress rating, e.g. getting married, having a baby or gaining a promotion. Good experiences usually entail a degree of change and it can be the changes to lifestyle and the need to develop new coping skills that contribute to the stress experienced.

Managing your stress

Don't wait for things to get better. Remember that you can always take *some* action to minimize, even if only by a small amount, the stress you feel.

Help yourself by coming to your own AID by:

Anticipating and planning for stressful activities.
Identifying the sources of your stress.
Developing coping strategies and practising them.

- Maintain or establish a strong support network. Research suggests that people who do so cope more easily with life and recover more quickly from setbacks.
- Accept your feelings and share them with others.
- Ask for help when you need it – and be gracious enough to accept it when it is offered. You may have offered help to other people and now it's your turn to accept help.
- You may need to undertake a life audit (see page 19) to identify what's wrong and what you need to do about it.

Relaxation

Relaxation plays an important part in coping with stress. Find time for yourself to:

- Enjoy a bath, light some candles, sprinkle a few drops of lavender aromatherapy oil into the water and take time for yourself.
- Play some gentle music, close your eyes and allow yourself time to relax.
- Enjoy your garden or local park, take time to look at the world around you.

Sleep

It is important for your psychological as well as physiological well-being to get the sleep you need. It can be difficult to remain confident when you are tired. Sleep is essential for survival and research suggests that the quality of sleep is more important than the quantity. Too little or too much can lead to poor performance and the amount of sleep required varies from person to person. Most people need seven hours, some nine and others only five.

It is often the worry about losing sleep that produces negative symptoms rather than the loss of sleep itself. Many people underestimate the amount of sleep they get, due to the time they spend worrying about not sleeping when they are awake.

The most important kind of sleep is what is called REM sleep or rapid eye movement, which is linked to dreaming. We all dream, even if we wake without any memory of dreaming.

Stress is a main cause of sleeping problems and people often lie awake at night worrying about problems or thinking about the future in a fearful way.

If you are experiencing sleep problems it can be helpful to:

- Keep to a routine. Have a warm milky drink, as milk contains tryptophan which aids sleep.
- Take a warm bath and use relaxing oils.
- Don't allow yourself to sleep during the day.
- Don't drink caffeine. Caffeine is a stimulant and can keep you awake at night. Too much coffee during the day may stop you from sleeping.
- Don't eat late at night.
- Get some exercise during the day. It can be helpful to take your exercise in the late afternoon or early evening.
- Use the relaxation exercises as outlined on page 78.
- Keep your sleeping environment as pleasant as possible.

My Stress Busting Action Plan

Think about each of the following questions and complete your Stress Busting Action Plan.

1 Which stress busting skills do I already feel competent in using?

_____

_____

_____

2 Which stress busting skills have I identified as needing work?

_____

_____

_____

3 Where and how am I going to practise my stress busting skills?

_____

_____

_____

4 How will I ensure I actually practise these skills? What might get in the way?

_____

_____

_____

5 What date will I put in my diary to check on my progress?

_____

The Confidence Diet

These days it is impossible to avoid information on healthy eating. However, what we eat also has an effect on our confidence levels and our ability to cope emotionally.

As was outlined in the stress busting section above, our bodies produce stress hormones and release fatty acids and sugars to help us cope with a perceived crisis. When such events take place our bodies' natural blood sugar levels are disturbed and this is also the case when we become angry or anxious. Our blood sugars help us regulate the fuel requirements needed by our body. Low blood sugar or hypoglycaemia contributes to symptoms of anxiety.

A drop in blood sugar causes reactions in the nervous system, including feelings of anxiety, confusion and panic attacks. Diets that contain large amounts of refined sugars or are deficient in protein or fat, together with the use of stimulants such as coffee or cola-based drinks, contribute to this condition.

Vitamin and mineral deficiencies also contribute to feelings of anxiety. You may be lacking in magnesium, zinc and the amino acid tryptophan. Alternatively, an excessive amount of some nutrients can speed up your nervous system and this can lead to feelings of anxiety. Potassium, sodium, phosphorus and copper are just such minerals.

If the thyroid or adrenal glands become overactive, such conditions affect the way we feel, as we cannot absorb and use sufficient minerals. As a result, anxiety may follow. An underactive thyroid is more likely to lead to feelings of depression than of anxiety.

What can I do to help myself?

If you have any concerns at all about your health, your first port of call should be your doctor. I have always believed that all medical conditions should be eliminated before considering any emotional and/or life factors.

The following are some dietary tips that will help you:

- Drink plenty of water – not only is it good for your skin, it helps flush out toxins and keeps your kidneys in good working order. Around eight large glasses a day is best. There is nothing wrong with adding flavourings if you are not keen on drinking plain water. However, avoid sugary flavourings as this will defeat the object. Drinking fruit teas is also a good way of getting water down you.
- Make sure you eat at least six times a day: breakfast, mid-morning, lunch, mid-afternoon, tea and dinner. By eating little and often and ensuring you do not skip meals you will help your blood sugar levels stay balanced.

- Keep healthy snacks around you and plan ahead for days when it may be difficult to find healthy meals.
- Try to avoid 'fast food' as it usually contains more fat and additives than are good for you.
- Take a multivitamin pill daily. It can be difficult to ensure you get all the nutrients you need through the food you eat and a multivitamin will help ensure you are topped up on any you may be missing.
- Try to avoid coffee, tea, cola drinks and chocolate as all these contain varying amounts of caffeine. It would be a sad world if you could not allow yourself a little of what you fancy, so if you want chocolate now and again buy the more expensive kind which has a higher concentration of cocoa solids and less sugar.
- Try to avoid saturated fats as these can lead to health problems. A diet that is high in fat will also contain high levels of cholesterol. There is an increased risk of cancer of the breast, colon and prostate as well as coronary heart disease.
- Try to avoid an excess of alcohol – alcohol dehydrates, is a depressant and can increase mood-swings, depressive symptoms and fuel aggression.
- Avoid excessive amounts of salt (sodium) as about a quarter of what we require is to be found naturally present in food. We require so little that we can quite happily survive on what occurs in our daily food.

What food should I eat?

The art is to eat as varied a diet as possible. However, the following provides you with a more detailed breakdown of a range of foods which contribute to good physical as well as psychological health.

Protein
- Meat, chicken
- Fish, shellfish
- Beans and pulses
- Soya products

Carbohydrates
Complex:
- Wholegrain bread
- Pasta

- Rice
- Peas and beans
- Vegetables
- Fruit and nuts

Refined (and not so helpful):
- Sweet foods

Calcium

- Milk, cheese, yogurt
- Fish
- Broccoli, spring greens, leeks, cabbage, parsnips, potatoes, blackberries and oranges

Potassium

- Potatoes and sweet potatoes
- Fish, sardines
- Pork, chicken
- Cauliflower, sweetcorn, avocados, leeks
- Breakfast cereals
- Natural yogurt
- Bananas, rhubarb

Iron

- Eggs
- Lean meat
- Wholegrain cereals
- Peas, beans, spinach, leeks, broccoli, spring greens, potatoes, avocados
- Dried fruit

Zinc and copper

- Liver and kidney, chicken
- Oysters
- Soya flour, cocoa powder
- Rice, bulgar wheat
- Beans, parsnips, plantain
- Pears

My Confidence Diet Action Plan

Think about each of the following questions and complete your Confidence Diet Action Plan.

1 Which foods and healthy eating habits do I already engage in?

_____

_____

_____

_____

2 Which foods and healthy eating habits do I need to now include in my daily life?

_____

_____

_____

_____

3 How will I ensure I actually make these changes – what might get in the way?

_____

_____

_____

_____

4 What date will I put in my diary to check on my progress?

_____

7
What If I Need More Help?

Many people do not understand what life coaching, counselling and psychotherapy involve, and how to choose an appropriate practitioner.

Life/business coaching

Life coaching is relatively new to the United Kingdom and although there are a few training organizations, there is not, as yet, a professional body to guide those in this field. It is therefore even more important when securing the services of a life coach that you check out his or her training and experience. You must always feel confident that the person you are seeing knows what they are doing and can help you.

A life or business coach is someone who is there to encourage you, to support you through difficult times, to help you build on your successes and design, plan and instigate successful business/life strategies. There are basically two types of coaching:

- *Business/executive coaching* involves helping you improve your performance at work. Business coaching could include helping you consider how to get the best out of your staff, your peers and your superiors, as well as helping you identify your strengths, weaknesses, opportunities and threats.
- *Life coaching* focuses in a more holistic way on any aspect of your life that you would like to improve. For example, a life coach could help you become more assertive with your friends and family, enable you to tackle people and situations you have avoided for fear of looking silly or being rejected, and help you overcome a personal block such as taking up a healthier lifestyle.

Although business and life coaching are seen as separate activities many people find they are linked. Sometimes what seems like a business problem may have a connection with other life factors.

Coaching is:

- practical
- skill-based
- individually tailored to each person's requirements
- fitted around your life and your needs
- result driven
- usually short term
- not a substitute for personal motivation – you still have to take responsibility for the problem, the changes you make and the amount of work you choose to do!

Unless a coach is trained in other types of therapy they will not have the skills to help you with more deeply rooted emotional problems. A good life coach will know when and where to refer you, should they believe you require more help than they are capable of giving.

Counselling and psychotherapy

The British Association for Counselling and Psychotherapy describes the nature of counselling as:

> The overall aim of counselling is to provide an opportunity for the client to work towards living in a way that he or she experiences as more satisfying and resourceful ... counselling may be concerned with developmental issues, addressing and resolving specific problems, making decisions, coping with crises, developing personal insight and knowledge, working through feelings of inner conflict or improving relationships with others. The counsellor's role is to facilitate the client's work in ways which respect the client's values, personal resources and capacity for choice within his or her cultural context.

The BACP's Code of Ethics and Practice for Counsellors goes on to say that:

> There is no generally accepted distinction between counselling and psychotherapy. There are well-founded traditions, which use the terms interchangeably and others which distinguish between them.

Counsellors and psychotherapy practitioners do not, unless medically qualified, prescribe any type of medication. Such practitioners work with a variety of clients and client problems.

The United Kingdom Council for Psychotherapy (UKCP) offers a UK-based register of psychotherapists. The UKCP represents a number of theoretical schools and each school has its own branch. Individuals belong to a specialist training organization or professional body representing one of the theoretical schools. Each practitioner will have demonstrated a baseline training and competency within that theoretical school to become eligible for registration. There are currently five branches within UKCP, these being psychoanalytic, humanistic and integrative, family, constructivist and cognitive-behavioural.

The British Association for Counselling and Psychotherapy also has a scheme to recognize the competence of counsellors. This is called accreditation. To become eligible for accreditation a counsellor has to have completed a minimum of 450 hours of basic training, have practical experience of a minimum of 450 client hours and meet a range of other professional requirements. The individual's application is then vetted, and if successful the applicant can then use the words *BACP Registered* or *Senior Registered Practitioner* after his or her name. Accredited counsellors have to demonstrate their commitment to maintaining and improving personal standards by engaging in a minimum of 30 hours' continued professional development annually.

In addition, a new register for counsellors has been set up in the UK called the United Kingdom Register of Counsellors.

The British Psychological Society (BPS) has its own recognition scheme, called *chartership*. A psychologist with additional specialist training in counselling can apply to become a chartered counselling psychologist.

There is a range of specialist professional bodies, such as the British Association for Behavioural and Cognitive Psychotherapies (BABCP), which also accredit psychotherapists. In this case you might see the words *BABCP Accredited Cognitive-Behavioural Psychotherapist* after the name of someone accredited with the BABCP. Most of these bodies also belong to UKCP.

Accreditation, registration and chartership minimize the chances of receiving inadequate help. However, therapists are human beings and people make mistakes.

In addition, counselling or psychotherapy may not always be the most appropriate form of help for an individual's problem. For example, a homeless person may find it helpful in a supportive way to talk to a counsellor. If his main problems are lack of money and poor accommodation he may be better off talking to an advice worker who could offer practical advice and support.

It's down to you!

Some people come to a life coach, counsellor or psychotherapist believing that the person concerned has a 'magic wand' to make everything right. Some people seem surprised that they have to take responsibility for doing exercises or homework assignments. It does not matter how well-trained, capable and good the counsellor is, it's up to you to do the work.

Get the most from the help on offer

Ask your practitioner to explain how he or she believes the particular type of help they offer will help you. If you are at all unsure or uncomfortable, then make the decision to find another person to work with you.

A good practitioner is able to:

- Offer an explanation of what is causing your problems in a way you will understand.
- Can give you some sense of how long you will need and what the process will involve. The style of working will reflect the person's training.

The following checklist was developed by Dr Stephen Palmer and Kasia Szymanska, at the Centre for Stress Management, London, for use when seeking a psychotherapist or counsellor.

- Check that your counsellor has relevant qualifications and experience in the field of counselling/psychotherapy.
- Ask about the type of approach the counsellor uses and how it relates to your problem.
- Ask if the counsellor is in clinical counselling supervision. (Most professional bodies consider supervision to be mandatory.)

- Ask if the counsellor or counselling agency is a member of a professional body and abides by the code of ethics. If possible, obtain a copy of the code.
- Discuss your goals and expectations.
- Ask about your counsellor's fee structure, if appropriate, and if you are on a low income check if the counsellor operates a sliding scale. Discuss the frequency and estimated duration of the counselling.
- Arrange regular review sessions with your counsellor to evaluate your progress.
- Do not enter into a long-term counselling contract unless you are satisfied that it is necessary and beneficial to you.

If you do not have a chance to discuss the above points during your first session, do so at the next possible opportunity.

In addition to the above, Palmer and Szymanska also discuss a number of other points:

- Counsellor self-disclosure can sometimes be therapeutically useful. If the sessions are dominated by the counsellor discussing his or her own problems at length this may not be appropriate and you should raise this issue in the counselling session. If at any time you feel discounted, undermined or manipulated within the session, discuss this with the counsellor too. It is easier to resolve issues as and when they arise.
- You should not accept significant gifts from your counsellor. This does not apply to relevant therapeutic material. Neither should you accept social invitations from your counsellor, e.g. dining in a restaurant or going for a drink. This does not apply to relevant therapeutic assignments, such as being accompanied by your counsellor into a situation to help you overcome a phobia.
- If your counsellor proposes a change in venue for the counselling sessions without good reason, e.g. a move from a centre to the counsellor's own home, do not agree unless you are totally satisfied with the reason for the move.
- Research has shown that it is not beneficial for clients to have sexual contact with their counsellor. Professional counselling and psychotherapy bodies consider it unethical for counsellors or therapists to engage in a sexual relationship with current clients.

If you have any doubts about the counselling you are receiving, then discuss them with your counsellor. If you are still uncertain, seek advice – perhaps from a friend, your doctor, your local Citizens' Advice Bureau, the professional body your counsellor belongs to or the counselling agency that may employ your counsellor. If you are still unsure that you and the therapist are the right fit, a sensible guideline is to commit to no more than two or three sessions to establish whether this is a person with whom you are comfortable. Remember that you have the right to terminate counselling whenever you choose.

The End

There is no reason why you should not get more of what you want from life. No one is saying it will always be easy. However, nothing ventured, nothing gained. Many people have turned their lives around and transformed themselves beyond recognition. Whether you want to make minor changes or more of a major overhaul, you are the one person that matters. You can do it – chip away a small amount on a daily basis and confidence and a better life can be yours.

I would like to know whether this book has been helpful to you and what other information you might benefit from knowing. Visit my website at *www.gladeana.com* and email me. Alternatively, do write to my publisher, who will forward your comments on to me.

To survive is not enough . . . to simply exist is not enough.
Star Trek, TNG

Useful Addresses

Ireland

Irish Association for Counselling and Therapy
8 Cumberland Street
Dun Laoghaire
Co Dublin
Tel. 01 230 0061
Provides information, advice and details of counselling services.

Irish Council for Psychotherapy
17 Dame Court
Dublin 2
Tel. 01 679 4055
Offers information, advice and details of services.

Scotland

COSCA (Confederation of Scottish Counselling Agencies)
64 Murray Place
Stirling FK8 2BX
Tel. 01786 475140
Professional body for counsellors in Scotland. Can provide details of
counsellors and information on counselling and counselling services.

United Kingdom

Association for Rational Emotive Behaviour Therapists
St George's
Winter Street
Sheffield S3 7ND
Tel. 0114 271 6926
Professional body for counsellors, psychologists and psychothera-
pists using REBT. Can provide details of such therapists.

British Association for Counselling and Psychotherapy
1 Regent Place
Rugby
Warwickshire CV21 2PJ
Tel. 01788 578 328
Professional body for counsellors in the UK. Can provide lists of counsellors and psychotherapists together with information.

British Association for Behavioural and Cognitive Psychotherapies
PO Box 9
Accrington BB5 2GD
Tel. 01254 875277
Professional body for psychiatrists, psychologists, counsellors and all those who use cognitive-behavioural techniques. Can provide lists of counsellors and also information on cognitive-behavioural psychotherapies.

British Psychological Society
St Andrew's House
48 Princess Road East
Leicester LE1 7DR
Tel. 0116 254 9568
Professional body for psychologists. Can also provide details of psychologists.

Centre for Coaching
156 Westcombe Hill
Blackheath
London SE3 7DH
Tel. 020 8293 4114
Provides certificated coaching courses and individual coaching programmes.

Centre for Stress Management
156 Westcombe Hill
Blackheath
London SE3 7DH
Tel. 020 8293 4114
Provides information and advice on stress-related issues together
with counselling and psychotherapy. Also offers training in a variety
of subjects, as well as Advanced Certificate and Diploma Courses in
Cognitive Behavioural Psychotherapy.

International Stress Management Association (UK)
Division of Psychology
South Bank University
103 Borough Road
London SE1 0AA
Tel. 07000 780430
Provides information, advice and details of stress management
practitioners and trainers.

UKCP (United Kingdom Council for Psychotherapy)
167 Great Portland Street
London W1N 5FB
Tel. 020 7436 3002
Register of psychotherapists in the UK.

UKRC (United Kingdom Register of Counsellors)
1 Regent Place
Rugby
Warwickshire CV21 2PJ
Tel. 01788 550899
Register of counsellors in the UK.

Europe

EAC (European Association for Counselling)
PO Box 82
Rugby
Warwickshire CV21 2AD
Tel. 01788 546731
Provides details of counselling organizations in Europe.

Index

ABC model 32, 35
achievements
  negative beliefs 50
  recording 70
actions
  action plan 111–12
  signs of stress 122
  see also assertiveness;
    problem-solving
alcohol 67
anger 65–6, 73–5
anxiety and worry 76–8
assertiveness 75
  features of 97–8
  managing put-downs 110–11
  other kinds of behaviour
    94–7
  saying 'yes' or 'no' 105–7
  skills 99–103
  three steps to 98–9
  training 92–4
attitudes
  discounting the positive
    38–9, 47
  optimism and pessimism
    30–1
avoidance 4

Beck, Aaron 32
beliefs, negative 49–51
blame and personalization
  negative thinking 40–1, 47–9
body language 10–13

understanding others 64
British Association for
    Behavioural and Cognitive
    Psychotherapies 133
British Association for
    Counselling and
    Psychotherapy 132–3
British Psychological Society
    133
business/executive coaching
    131–2

catastrophizing 43, 49, 50
  shame and humiliation 75
Churchill, Winston 30
cognitive-behaviour therapy 5
Collins, J. Churton 59
confidence
  action plan 21–2
  feelings action plan 83–4
  symptoms of lacking 6–7
conflict
  coping with 103–5
  see also assertiveness
conversation
closed and open questions
    14–15
  listening 16–17
  making small talk 13
cost-benefit analysis 72–3
counselling 132–6
criticism
  believing in failure 50
  giving 108–10

143